IMAGES OF WAR

RUSSIAN ARMOUR in the SECOND WORLD WAR

RARE PHOTOGRAPHS FROM WARTIME ARCHIVES

MICHAEL GREEN

Pen & Sword
MILITARY

First published in Great Britain in 2013 by
PEN & SWORD MILITARY
an imprint of
Pen & Sword Books Ltd
47 Church Street
Barnsley
South Yorkshire
S70 2AS

ISBN 978 1 78159 183 3

Typeset in Gill Sans

Printed and bound in India by
Replika Press Pvt. Ltd.

Pen & Sword Books Ltd incorporates the Imprints of Pen & Sword Aviation, Pen & Sword Family History, Pen & Sword Maritime, Pen & Sword Military, Pen & Sword Discovery, Wharncliffe Local History, Wharncliffe True Crime, Wharncliffe Transport, Pen & Sword Select, Pen & Sword Military Classics, Leo Cooper, The Praetorian Press, Remember When, Seaforth Publishing and Frontline Publishing

For a complete list of Pen & Sword titles please contact
PEN & SWORD BOOKS LIMITED
47 Church Street, Barnsley, South Yorkshire, S70 2AS, England
E-mail: enquiries@pen-and-sword.co.uk
Website: www.pen-and-sword.co.uk

Contents

Acknowledgments

I could not have completed this book without a number of long-time friends taking the time to dig through their photo files (be it a shoe box or digital) to retrieve pictures for me to include. Their names are found in the photo credits. A special word of thanks goes to Bob Fleming for the sheer number of historical photographs he supplied to me. The individual quality of the pictures in this book varies widely, reflecting the large number of different sources and time periods encompassed by the photographs.

My good friend and fellow author Chris Hughes took it upon himself to climb inside a variety of cramped and uncomfortable vehicles to shoot interior photographs for this book. Other friends who did not contribute pictures but took the time to read and review my text and captions include Michael Panchyshyn, Chun-Lun Hsu, Yuri Desyatnik and James D. Brown.

Institutions that assisted the author include the Military Vehicle Technology Foundation and its late director Philip Hatcher. There was also David Fletcher of the Tank Museum, Bovington, England, who spent many hours looking through their photo files for me. Pictures credited to the Tank Museum, Bovington are shortened to just Tank Museum for the sake of brevity. Lastly, I wish to thank the very helpful staff of the now-closed Patton Museum of Cavalry and Armor for their assistance through the many years. Picture credits to that museum are shortened to just the Patton Museum.

Dedication

I would like to dedicate this book to my good friend Vladimir Yakubov for all his help on this one and many others.

Introduction

Starting with almost nothing in 1919, except for a small number of British and French-made tanks captured from White Russian forces and a handful of armoured cars, by the early 1930s the Red Army was one of the leaders in the innovative use of large armoured forces. Sadly, by the late 1930s, the Red Army was being shaken by bloody purges that did away with its more inventive tank-minded military thinkers. These purges had been ordered by Stalin to clear the way for a generation of more politically reliable – but which would later prove to be militarily incompetent – functionaries.

The murder by Stalin of many of the most forward thinkers in the Red Army officer corps would come back to haunt him with the German military invasion of the Soviet Union in June 1941. Despite having the largest fleet of tanks in the world, estimated at over 22,000 vehicles, more than the rest of the world combined, the Red Army proved itself woefully ill-prepared to deal with the approximately 5,000 German tanks advancing into the Russian hinterland.

The Soviet inability to halt the German tanks can be attributed to poor leadership at the most senior military levels of the Red Army that had left their massive inventory of tanks in a near total state of disrepair with shortages of everything from parts and fuel to ammunition. It was these shortcomings, and many others such as a faulty doctrine, that allowed the German panzer arm to generally prevail on the battlefield over their much more numerous opponents in spite of occasional tactical setbacks.

The Red Army would lose nearly 90 per cent of its tanks between June 1941 and December 1941. However, it was those losses that helped to blunt and eventually bring the German tanks to a halt just outside the gates to Moscow. By way of comparison, the German army would lose over half of its tanks during the same time period.

There was a hidden benefit to the huge losses in tanks suffered by the Red Army in 1941. It helped to clear out the bulk of their pre-war tank fleet, with the majority of these being derivatives of old British and American technology. These vehicles were already obsolete by the standards of the day and paved the way for the large-scale introduction of a generation of new, more capable tanks and other armoured fighting vehicles that would eventually form the basis of one of the largest and most powerful armies ever fielded in the history of the world.

The new Red Army tanks and armoured fighting vehicles were not individually better than their late-war German counterparts because that was never the

Russian intention, but they were good enough and eventually available in sufficient numbers to successfully counter any German qualitative superiority. It was these large numbers that also made up for the continued high battlefield losses suffered by the Red Army in combat with its German opponent throughout the Second World War.

If you add up all the light, medium and heavy tanks constructed in Soviet factories during the Second World War you get a total number built of 76,827 vehicles. By way of comparison, German industry only managed to build approximately 24,000 tanks during the same time period – not counting self-propelled guns – which needed to be dispersed over multiple theatres of war. The most numerous German tank built was the Panzer IV series of medium tanks with about 9,000 units being assembled; in comparison the most numerous Soviet tank design was the T-34 series with nearly 58,000 built. It was this Russian policy of outbuilding their enemies in the Second World War that is exemplified by the maxim (attributed to a great many authors) that 'Quantity has a quality all its own.'

The T-34 series formed the bulk of the Red Army tank inventory from 1943 through to 1945. While the workmanship on the vehicle may not have been up to German standards and many who had a chance to study the vehicle considered some of the tank's construction shoddy, it was 'good enough' for the battlefields of the Eastern Front. On the positive side, the T-34 series mounted versatile cannons, were relatively easy to build in large numbers, simple to maintain in the field, and had enough reliability to make it to the battlefield in large enough numbers to overwhelm its opponents.

This book is not intended to be a comprehensive study of Russian armour in the Second World War; rather your author has attempted to provide the reader with a broad pictorial survey of the subject. Accompanying the photographs are relevant text and captions to assist the reader in placing the vehicles shown in historical context.

Note to the readers:

Unlike other armies before and during the Second World War, the Red Army did not have a consistent policy of assigning designations to the various subvariants of their tanks and other armoured fighting vehicles. Post-war historians and authors have in response developed a practice of assigning model numbers to Red Army tanks and armoured fighting vehicles based on the year they were introduced into service in order to distinguish between subvariants. This practice has been adopted by the author to assist the reader in identifying the often many different versions of vehicles produced. However, rebuilt vehicles or field modifications may result in a mixture of subvariant features that do not fit into any classification.

Chapter One

Light Tanks

The Russian Imperial Army did not field any tanks in the First World War (1914–18). However, after the fall of the Russian Royal Family in the spring of 1917 and the resultant rise to power of the Bolsheviks under Vladimir Lenin, anti-Bolshevik forces aligned with the former Tsarist regime were

Pictured is a French-designed and built two-man Renault FT-17 light tank armed with a 37mm main gun. The Red Army captured a number of these tanks in its early years from the anti-Bolshevik forces, called the 'Whites', during a bloody civil war that raged from 1917–1924. (*Pierre-Olivier B.*)

Belonging to the Military Museum of the Army of France located in Paris, France is this Renault FT-17. The anti-Bolshevik Whites received the Renault FT-17 and other tanks due to the support they had from the French and British governments who feared the spread of the new Communist ideology. (*Christophe Vallier*)

supplied a wide variety of military equipment, including tanks, from the British and French army inventories.

One of the tank types provided by the Western Allies to the anti-Bolshevik forces was the two-man, French-designed and built Renault FT-17 light tank which first saw combat in France against the German army in 1918. It was either armed with a single turret-mounted 7.92mm machine gun or a short-barrelled 37mm cannon. The gasoline-engine-powered Renault FT-17 weighed 15,432lb (7mt) and had a maximum armour thickness of 22mm on the front of the turret, typically the thickest armour on all tanks.

During the bloody civil war (1917–24) that raged between the Bolsheviks and anti-Bolshevik forces referred to as the 'Whites', a small number of Renault

FT-17 light tanks fell into the hands of the 'Red Army', the military wing of the Bolshevik Party, which had been formed in January 1918. The Red Army did not become the Soviet Army until 25 February 1946.

In Red Army service the captured French Renault FT-17 light tanks were referred to as the 'Reno'. The captured White Army Reno tanks and the other larger and heavier medium and heavy tanks acquired by the Red Army contributed little to its overall success during the civil war; however, these vehicles constituted the beginning of its armoured forces in 1919.

To build up their tank strength during the bitter civil war the senior military leadership of the Red Army decided to have the French-designed Renault FT-17 light tank reverse-engineered. The first example of this was completed by August 1920. After three months of testing, the vehicle received several different names.

Part of the collection of the Royal Museum of the Armed Forces and of Military History located in Brussels, Belgium is this Renault FT-17. Despite the capture of some French and British tanks by the Red Army, the small number of vehicles involved meant they would play only a minor role in the Red Army's eventual defeat of the Whites. (*Michel Krauss*)

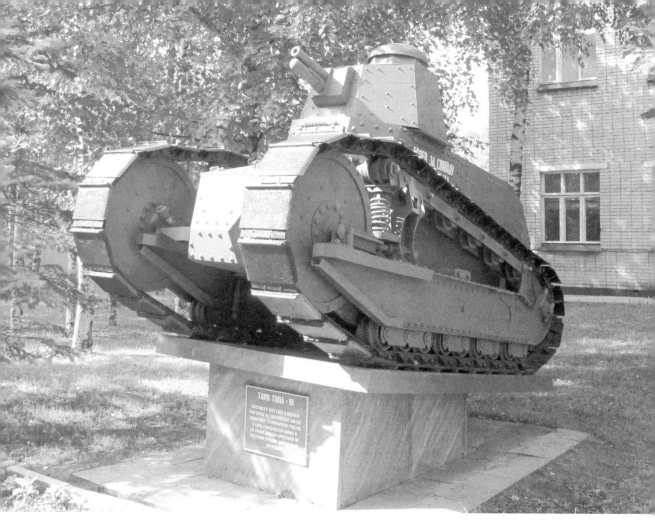

On display at the War History Museum of Armoured Vehicles and Equipment located in the outskirts of Moscow, Russia, most often referred to as Kubinka, is a surviving example of a Red Army reverse-engineered copy of the Renault FT-17. Various sources list fifteen vehicles as being completed between 1921 and 1922. (*Vladimir Yakubov*)

These included the *Russkiy* Reno, the *Legkiy* tank KS, or the most public-relations-oriented version, the 'Freedom Fighter Lenin' tank. It is believed that the Red Army had fourteen additional examples built of the reverse-engineered FT-17s.

The Soviet Union undertook a massive policy of industrialization beginning in the 1920s through to the early 1930s that included the purchase of large amounts of foreign-made industrial machinery for the building of everything from cars to tractors. This was done to acquire the infrastructure needed to manufacture tanks in large numbers. The first tank to roll off the new factory assembly lines in 1928 was the gasoline-engine-powered two-man T-18 light tank also known as the MS-1 (*Maliy Soprovozhdyeniya-Pierviy*, which translates as the 'First Small Support Vehicle').

Part of the Kubinka collection is this Red Army T-18 light tank, also referred to as the MS-1, which was based on the design of the Renault FT-17 with a new Russian-designed suspension system. It was armed with a turret-mounted 37mm main gun and two 7.62mm machine guns in a separate gun mount. The suspension system shown is a post-war reconstruction. (*Bob Fleming*)

Derived from the Renault FT-17 light tank with a Russian-designed suspension system to improve its cross-country performance, series production of the T-18 light tank began in 1928 and continued until 1931 with approximately 959 units being completed. The vehicle originally mounted a slightly improved version of the original French-designed and built 37mm main gun. Instead of a coaxial machine gun it had a 7.62mm machine gun in a separate mount in the right front of the turret. The 14,770-lb (6.7mt) vehicle first saw combat during the Sino-Soviet conflict of 1929.

Reflecting the embryonic nature of tank design in the Soviet Union during this time period, the T-18 light tank was plagued by numerous early design issues. Nevertheless, the building of this tank in such large numbers was an incredible achievement for a country that had just transitioned from being almost strictly an agriculturally-based economy a few years earlier.

There was a plan at one point to modernize the T-18 and turn it into the T-18M with a new engine and 37mm main gun, but it was deemed too expensive and only one example was ever built. The suffix 'M' was an abbreviation of the Russian word *modifitsirovanniy* that translates as 'modified'. A few T-18 tanks were later up-armed with a 45mm main gun in 1932.

Because of deficiencies in engineering talent and industrial capacity, the Red Army continued to look at acquiring foreign-designed armoured vehicles for inspiration from the late 1920s up until 1940. Among the various British-designed tanks purchased and brought to the Soviet Union for technical evaluation was the two-man Carden Loyd Mark VI Tankette, built and marketed by the civilian firm of Vickers-Armstrong. By today's standards the 3,360-lb (1.5mt) vehicle would be considered a light tank; however, the term 'tankette' was a popular name during the interwar period when referring to these extremely small one or two-man turretless machine-gun-armed vehicles.

The Red Army decided in February 1931 that the Carden Loyd Mark VI Tankette would be suitable as an infantry support and reconnaissance vehicle. It

The influence of the Renault FT-17 design can be clearly seen in this view of a Red Army T-18 located at Kubinka as it features a tail beam, just like the French tank, intended to prevent it from tipping over when exiting a trench. The T-18 was built between 1928 and 1931. The suspension system pictured is a post-war reconstruction. (*Bob Fleming*)

Another T-18 on display at Kubinka features a different arrangement of 37mm main gun and a single 7.62mm machine gun. T-18 tank turrets employed as pillboxes by the Red Army were up-gunned with a turret armed with a 45mm main gun and no machine guns. (*Vladimir Yakubov*)

was therefore ordered that a Soviet-built, two-man copy be placed into production to be armed with a single 7.62mm machine gun and have overhead armour. Before production began the vehicle was redesigned to improve its performance. The first of these improved 5,952-lb (2.7mt) tankettes rolled off the factory floor at the end of 1931 and was designated the T-27.

Maximum armour thickness on the turretless T-27 series was 10mm on the front hull. By the time production ended in 1933 a total of 3,328 units had been completed. This number included 187 units armed with a flame-thrower gun in lieu of the standard 7.62mm machine gun.

The Red Army originally envisioned that it would field an inventory of 5,000 units of the T-27 tankette series. However, it soon became clear that the vehicle had limited combat effectiveness because it was under-gunned, under-armoured and had poor off-road mobility. As a result, production of the T-27 tankette

Looking for inspiration from design work being done in Great Britain, the Red Army bought a single example of a two-man Vickers Carden Loyd Mark VI tankette in 1929. The model pictured here is armed with a 7.7mm machine gun. The Red Army liked what they saw, made some automotive improvements to the design, and placed it into production as the T-27 in 1931. (*Tank Museum*)

series was ended prematurely. Many of these vehicles went on to have a second career as training vehicles or prime movers for small towed anti-tank guns as their usefulness as infantry support or reconnaissance vehicles in the Red Army came to an end.

The Red Army had also bought examples of the two-man machine-gun-armed Vickers-Armstrong Carden Loyd Amphibious Tank, Model 1931. It seemed the idea of an amphibious reconnaissance tank caught the imagination of the Red Army and they used the British vehicle as a starting point to develop their own two-man vehicle as a replacement for the T-27 tankette series. The new vehicle was designated the T-37A. It weighed 7,055lb (3.2mt), was gasoline-powered and had a maximum armour thickness of 9mm on its front of its turret.

Some 1,954 units of the machine-gun-armed T-37A were built between 1933 and 1936, and there were seventy-five units built with a flame-thrower gun. Also constructed were 673 radio-equipped command vehicles, designated the

T-37RT, the suffix 'RT' standing for radio tank. The command version of the T-37A could be identified by its hull-mounted metal frame antenna. Radios did not become standard equipment in Red Army tanks until late in the Second World War.

There was a remote-controlled version of the T-37A that had the suffix 'TT' for *Teletank* in its designation. Directing the remote-control tanks was the *Tank Upravleniya* guidance (or command) tank that was shortened to the suffix 'TU' in the vehicle's designation.

A modernized version of the T-37A that had a wider and lower hull received the designation T-38. The 7,392-lb (3.3mt) vehicle was in production between 1936 and 1937 with 1,228 units completed. Maximum armour thickness on the front of the turret was 9mm. The standard weapon for both the T-37 and the T-38 series was a turret-mounted 7.62mm machine gun. One or two proto-type T-38 series tanks were armed with the 20mm automatic cannon in place of their standard 7.62mm machine gun and designated the T-38Sh.

The T-38 would see combat in the Russo-Finnish War (November 1939–March 1940) and the first few months of 1941 during the German invasion of the Soviet Union along with the T-37. Rather than seeing use as amphibious

The Red Army T-27 tankette differed in some external details from its Vickers Carden Loyd Mark VI counterpart. Instead of two separate overhead hatches there was now only a single large hatch for the two-man crew. The suspension system on each side of the hull had three bogie assemblies instead of the two seen on the British vehicle. (*Bob Fleming*)

Shown in a Russian repair shop are two T-27 tankettes. The Red Army eventually concluded that the vehicles were unsuitable as reconnaissance vehicles, being under-gunned and under-armoured with poor off-road mobility. Most were eventually reassigned as prime movers for towed anti-tank guns. (*Bob Fleming*)

reconnaissance vehicles, their primary role became infantry support. Some would survive until July 1944 during the crossing of the river Syir where all the surviving T-37A and T-38 tanks, a total of forty vehicles, were used in the first assault wave.

Never stopping for long to improve their tank inventory, the Red Army had sought out a replacement for the T-38 years before the German invasion. That tank was approved for production in December 1939 as the T-40 Model 1940 Amphibious Tank. The two-man gasoline-engine-powered T-40 weighed 12,324lb (5.6mt) and was the first Red Army tank to feature a torsion bar suspension system. The maximum armour thickness on the front of the vehicle's turret was 14mm.

The T-40 was armed with a turret-mounted 12.7mm machine gun and a coaxial 7.62mm machine gun. A total of 221 units of the T-40 came off the assembly line before the German invasion of the Soviet Union. There was also a non-amphibious version of the T-40 put into production shortly after the German invasion. It was designated the T-40S and 136 were constructed between July and September 1941. The suffix 'S' *Sukhoputnyj* is the Russian term for land-operated. Forty-four T-40s, minus turrets, were converted to mount a version of the *Katyusha* rocket-launchers, normally seen mounted on wheeled vehicles.

Another non-amphibious version of the T-40 started coming off the factory floors in August 1941. It featured thicker armour than the original T-40 and eventually appeared with a turret-mounted 20mm automatic cannon in place of the 12.7mm machine gun. It retained the 7.62mm coaxial machine gun. Reflecting the changes to the vehicle design it was re-designated as the T-30S and a total of 335 units were completed between August and October 1941.

Before the German invasion of the Soviet Union, the Red Army had yet another two-man light tank design in the works. It was designated the T-60 Model 1941 light tank and was armed with a turret-mounted 20mm automatic cannon and a coaxial 7.62mm machine gun. About the same size as the T-40, the gasoline-powered T-60 weighed 11,354lb (5.1mt) and was never intended to have any amphibious capability, making it faster and cheaper to build. The maximum armour protection on the front of the vehicle's turret was originally

The Red Army obtained a small number of British-designed and built amphibious light tanks in 1931. They used the British vehicles as a base upon which to come up with their own two-man amphibious light tank designated the T-37A, an example of which is seen here in the water. (*Bob Fleming*)

Pictured is a column of T-37A tanks led by a radio-equipped command version with its frame antenna. The radio command vehicle was designated as the T-37RT. The only armament on the vehicle was a single turret-mounted 7.62mm machine gun. The maximum land speed of the T-37A was 23.6 mph. (*Bob Fleming*)

Two Red Army T-37A amphibious tanks are shown crossing a river. The vehicle was 12ft 4in (3.75m) long, 6ft 7in (2m) wide and 5ft 11in (1.8m) tall. It was armed with a single turret-mounted 7.62mm machine gun. (*Bob Fleming*)

25mm, later increased to 35mm, making it also better protected than previous amphibious-capable tanks.

Production of the T-60 Model 1941 began in July 1941. It was soon followed by an improved version designated the T-60 Model 1942 that had a more powerful engine. Production of the T-60 series ended in September 1942 in favour of the next-generation light tank with 6,022 units completed. As with the T-40S, a number of turretless T-60s were modified to mount a version of the *Katyusha* rocket-launcher.

The planned replacement for the T-60 series was the up-armoured 21,958-lb (10mt) T-70 Model 1942 light tank. Maximum armour protection on the front of the vehicle's turret was 50mm. The two-man gasoline-engine-powered vehicle was armed with a turret-mounted 45mm tank gun and a coaxial 7.62mm machine gun. As the original T-70 had some design problems it was redesigned with an improved suspension system, wider tracks and stronger torsion bars. The T-70M had storage space for seventy main gun rounds versus ninety for the original version of the vehicle.

Production of the T-70M began in March 1942 and continued until October 1943 with 8,226 units completed. There was a redesigned version of the T-70M built that featured a two-man turret and was referred to as the T-80. It had a maximum armour thickness of 45mm on the front of the turret. However, by the time the 25,984-lb (11.8mt) T-80 entered production it was clear to the Red

Field use of the T-37A amphibious tank showed it to have a number of design shortcomings. To address these complaints, efforts were undertaken in 1934 to redesign the vehicle. The end result was the production, beginning in 1936, of the T-38 amphibious light tank seen here during a pre-Second World War parade. (*Bob Fleming*)

Army that light tanks had no place on the battlefield and production ended after only seventy-seven units were built, not counting two prototypes.

Among the many British tanks acquired pre-war by the Red Army was the gasoline-engine-powered twin-turreted Vickers-Armstrong 13,440-lb (6.1mt) E light tank. The three-man tank made a favourable impression during testing and an improved licence-built copy featuring a twin-turret machine-gun arrangement was authorized for production by the Red Army. The new 20,608-lb (9.3mt) light tank was intended as an infantry support vehicle and was designated the T-26 Model 1931.

The T-26 Model 1931 was armed with two 7.62mm machine guns, one in each turret. Production took place between 1931 and 1934 with 1,627 units completed. A radio-equipped command version of this vehicle with its right side turret armed with a 37mm main gun was designated the T-26RT Model 1931. As with the T-37A there was a remote-control version of the tank with the suffix 'TT' in its designation and their command vehicles having the suffix 'TU'. Maximum armour thickness on the front of the vehicle's turret was 15mm.

In 1932 the Red Army ordered that a 45mm gun be mounted in a T-26 light tank fitted with a larger two-man turret. The new tank gun was based on an up-scaled version of a German-designed 37mm towed anti-tank that the Red Army had purchased the rights to licence-build in the Soviet Union. With this new turret and the 45mm main gun, the 22,927-lb (10.4mt) vehicle was designated the T-26 Model 1933. This would prove to be the most numerous model of the T-26 series built, with 5,500 units completed between 1933 and 1936. An improved 45mm main gun was installed in the T-26 Model 1933 starting in 1935.

Combat experience gained during the Spanish Civil War (July 1936–April 1939) showed the 45mm-gun-equipped T-26 Model 1933 light tanks supplied to the Republican side on Stalin's orders were far superior to the machine-gun-armed light tanks and tankettes supplied by the German and Italian governments to the Nationalist side. The thin armour protection on the T-26 Model 1933, however, proved to be its Achilles' heel against the German-supplied 37mm towed anti-tanks provided to the Nationalists as many were lost to this foe. In total, the Soviet Union supplied the Republican side with 281 units of the T-26 Model 1933 light tank.

The first three rows of vehicles shown are the T-38 amphibious tank with the following rows being the T-37A. The turret of the T-38 was on the left-hand side of the hull and the driver on the right-hand side, the reverse of that on the T-37A. (*Bob Fleming*)

Pictured during pre-Second World War training manoeuvres is a column of T-38 amphibious tanks. The one-man 7.62mm machine-gun-armed turret on the vehicle was a slightly redesigned version of that mounted on the T-37A. The T-38 lacked the thicker cork-filled fenders seen on the T-37A. (*Bob Fleming*)

It was during the series production run of the T-26 Model 1933 light tank that the Red Army opted to use welding in the tank's construction rather than riveting, due to the superior ballistic protection it offered. The impetus for this change occurred because the riveted version of the T-26 Model 1933 tank had proven to be ballistically deficient during the border fighting that took place between the Red Army and Japanese army units based in Manchuria in 1938 and 1939.

Following on the heels of the T-26 Model 1933 tank appeared a series of progressively improved versions of the vehicle almost yearly. The T-26 Model 1938 and follow-on tanks continued to be armed with 45mm main guns. These tanks would remain in production until 1941 and feature redesigned turrets and hulls offering a superior level of protection to their predecessors, with a maximum armour thickness on the front of their turrets of 20mm.

Despite the increase in armour protection on the later production models of the T-26 series, combat experience during the Russo-Finnish War showed this remained inadequate and the Red Army had a small number of these vehicles provided with add-on armour for both their turrets and hulls. The Red Army had no special designation for the up-armoured T-26 tanks, but if it had it would have been 'Eh' for the Russian letter 'Э', the abbreviation for the Russian word *ekranirovannyj* – 'appliqued'.

The T-26 light tank series came in a number of different variants besides T-26RT command tanks, which often featured metal frame antennas around their turrets or hulls. These included a bridge-launcher version designated the ST-26 (*Sapernyj Tank*: Engineer Tank). Like the T37A there was also a remote-controlled version of the T-26 that had the suffix 'TT' for *teletank* in its

On display at the Central Armed Forces Museum in Moscow, Russia is this up-gunned example of the T-38 amphibious tank armed with a turret-mounted 20mm cannon. The T-38 did not prove to be much of an improvement over the T-37A in field service and its production was stopped in 1937. (*Vladimir Yakubov*)

Shown is a Red Army T-40 amphibious tank captured by the German army. It has been marked with the thickness of the various armour plates that made up the vehicle. The T-40 was the planned replacement for the T-37A and T-38 amphibious light tanks. (*Patton Museum*)

designation, while the command vehicles for the remote-control tanks had the suffix 'TU' included in their designation.

Some T-26 series light tanks were modified as artillery prime movers and assigned the designation T-26T. A total of 197 units of the turretless T-26T were produced. There were also the Su-5-1 (76mm), Su-5-2 (122mm) and Su-5-3 (152mm) self-propelled guns, as well as the TR-26 armoured personnel carrier, TV-26 ammo-transporter and T-26Ts fuel transporter, all built in small numbers.

The most numerous variant of the T-26 series was the flame-thrower version which constituted 12 per cent of the total number of vehicles built. The flame-thrower versions of the T-26 light tank featured different designations, with the original based on the T-26 Model 1931 referred to as the KhT-26, with the flame gun mounted in a single turret on the right side, with the left turret removed. The prefix 'KhT' is the abbreviation for the Russian term *Khimicheskiy Tank*, which translates as 'chemical tank'. Post-war publications sometimes used the prefix 'OT', the abbreviation for the Russian words *Ognemetniy Tank* which translates as 'flame-throwing tank'. In addition to the KhT-26, there were the

The T-40's main armament was a turret-mounted 12.7mm machine gun as seen in this close-up photograph of the vehicle's turret. Not seen in this picture is the coaxial 7.62mm machine gun. The vehicle carried 500 rounds of 12.7mm ammunition and 2,061 rounds of 7.62mm ammunition. (*Patton Museum*)

OT-130, 131, 132, 133 and 134 built in significant numbers with different turret/flame-thrower/machine-gun arrangements.

In total, the Red Army would take into service about 11,000 units of the T-26 series between 1931 and 1941. They would represent the bulk of the Red Army inventory of tanks based in the western military districts that faced the German army when their invasion of the Soviet Union began in the summer of 1941. The T-26 series of light tanks would continue to see service in ever-diminishing numbers with the Red Army up until the conclusion of the Second World War.

Before the German invasion of the Soviet Union, the Red Army had sought a replacement for the T-26 series in the infantry support role. What eventually appeared was the four-man, diesel-engine-powered T-50 light tank armed with a 45mm main gun. It was strictly an indigenous design and had many advanced features for its time, such as a torsion bar suspension system and three-man turret crew, in contrast to the one or two-man turret crews on other Red Army light tanks of the time. Sadly, the T-50 proved more complicated and costly to

One of the two-man crew of a T-40 amphibious tank is shown posing in front of his vehicle. Design work on this model had begun in 1938 with production starting in 1940 and continuing up until mid-1941. It was the first Red Army tank to have a torsion bar suspension system. (*Bob Fleming*)

build than anticipated and only sixty-three units were completed before series production was cancelled in February 1942. Maximum armour protection on the 30,864-lb (14mt) T-50 was 37mm on the front of its turret.

Besides legitimately acquiring a number of British tank designs during the 1930s for study, the Red Army was not averse to using subterfuge if there was a foreign tank design that proved of interest to them. A series of prototype tank designs that had sprung forth from the fertile imagination of American inventor J. Walter Christie drew the Red Army's interest. His prototype gasoline-engine-powered tanks had a suspension system based on helically-wound coil springs acting independently on large road wheels. This innovative new suspension system allowed his prototype tanks to reach unheard-of speeds for their day.

Another innovative feature of Christie's designs that attracted the attention of the Red Army was his development of a convertible track system. In this context, the term 'convertible' meant that a tank would run on its tracks when travelling off-road, but have its tracks removed when running on paved roads, operating only on its large, rubber-rimmed road wheels. The need for a tank to be able to operate without its tracks reflected the very short lifespan of track designs at that time.

With the collusion of Christie, the Red Army then bought two examples of one of his numerous designs, in this case the M1930 Convertible tank. They were shipped to the Soviet Union in December 1930 without their turrets and labelled as agricultural tractors. Christie's arrangement with the Red Army had not gone unnoticed and there were some efforts by the United States army War Department and the State Department to block the sale, all to no avail.

Upon arrival in the Soviet Union, the two M1930 tanks were quickly copied. The Red Army's first production version of Christie's convertible tank was

Production of the T-40 amphibious tank ended with the German invasion of the Soviet Union in June 1941 and a non-amphibious version was built instead, referred to as the T-30. Later production units of the vehicle were armed with a turret-mounted 20mm gun as seen on this example on display at Kubinka. (*Vladimir Yakubov*)

Pictured is a two-man T-60 light tank. It was based on the powertrain and suspension system of the T-40 amphibious tank with a more compact and streamlined up-armoured hull and turret. The T-60 was armed with a 20mm automatic cannon and a coaxial 7.62mm machine gun. (*Patton Museum*)

designated the BT-2 Model 1932. The prefix 'BT' is an abbreviation for the Russian words *Bystrokhodnyj Tank* that translated means 'fast tank' or 'high-speed tank'. It took a well-trained crew about half an hour to remove the tracks from the BT-2 and about the same amount of time to place them back on the vehicle.

The early production units of the BT-2 were armed with twin 7.62mm machine guns in the front of the turret and an additional 7.62mm machine gun in a ball mount at the right front of the turret. The original intention was to mount a 37mm main gun in the BT-2 turret. However, production problems with the 37mm gun forced the Red Army to make do with the twin 7.62mm machine-gun arrangement until such time as these issues were resolved. Once the production bottleneck for the 37mm guns was overcome all BT-2 tanks began appearing with this main gun and most of the early production units of the tank were later retrofitted with it. The armour protection for the BT-2 was limited to a maximum of 13mm on the front of the turret.

With lessons learned from construction of the BT-2, the next version in the series that came off the assembly lines was the 25,352-lb (11.5mt) BT-5 Model 1932. It featured a larger turret armed with a 45mm main gun and dispensed

This photograph shows two Red Army tankers conferring on the side of a T-60 tank as is evident by its distinctive gun shield. The vehicle was 13ft 5in (4.1m) long, 14ft 11in (4.5m) wide and 5ft 6in (1.7m) tall. (*Bob Fleming*)

with the ball-mounted 7.62mm machine gun fitted in the right front of the turret. In its place was a coaxial 7.62mm machine gun. An easily spotted external feature that allows one to distinguish between the BT-2 and the BT-5 was their respective turret designs. The front of the BT-2 turret roof was sloped and there was no turret bustle, while the BT-5 turret roof was flat with a turret bustle.

The replacement for the BT-5 would be the 31,360-lb (15.7mt) BT-7 Model 1935, which retained the layout of the BT-5's turret but differed from its predecessor because it had a redesigned hull and turret of all welded construction rather than the riveted construction seen on the BT-5. A noticeable external feature that allows one to distinguish between the very similar-looking tanks was that the BT-7 front hull is rounded while the BT-5 front hull came to a squared point. Unlike the exposed mufflers on the BT-5, the mufflers on the rear hull on the BT-7 were enclosed.

An important internal change on the BT-7 was the replacement of the Red Army copy of the American-designed and built gasoline-powered Liberty engine that powered the BT-2 and BT-5 with a more powerful gasoline-powered engine that was a copy of a German-designed and built engine. In 1937, with the

Two Red Army T-60 tanks are on the way to the front. Armour thickness on the front hull of the vehicle originally topped out at 20mm, with the hull sides being 15mm thick. Late production units of the T-60 had their front hull armour increased to 35mm and the hull sides up to 25mm. (*Bob Fleming*)

introduction of a new turret with sloped armour, the vehicle was re-designated as the BT-7 Model 1937.

Some late-model production BT-7 Model 1937 tanks were fitted with a 7.62mm machine gun in a ball mount in the rear turret bustle. A command version of the BT-7 Model 1937 was designated the BT-7RT and many were fitted with a more modern whip antenna rather than the old-fashioned metal frame antenna commonly seen on other pre-war Red Army command tanks.

The final version of the BT series, designated the BT-7M, was nearly identical to the late production BT-7 Model 1937 with some minor differences. These included redesigned hatches on the top of the vehicle's turret that allowed for a ring mount, designated P-40, with a 7.62mm machine gun for anti-aircraft protection. The vehicle was sometimes referred to unofficially as the BT-8.

Pictured on display at Kubinka is this T-60 tank. The gas-operated automatic cannon on the vehicle was designated the 20mm TNSh-1 and based on the design of an aircraft weapon that first appeared in production in 1936. (*Vladimir Yakubov*)

The biggest internal change to the BT-7M was a diesel-powered engine that greatly increased the maximum operational range of the vehicle due to the greater thermal efficiency of diesel fuel over gasoline fuel. Diesel fuel is also a great deal less flammable than gasoline fuel and therefore provided a safer tank for its crew. Increased protection for the crew also came from the up-armouring of the BT-7M to a maximum armour thickness of 22mm on the front of its turret. Due to this modification, the BT-7M lost its ability to run on wheels.

Production of the BT-7M ended in 1941. The figures for the number of BT series tanks built vary from a low of 7,000 to as many as 11,000 depending on the sources quoted. At least fifty units of the BT-5 were supplied to the Republican side under Stalin's orders and saw combat during the hard-fought Spanish Civil War. Both the Red Army's BT-5s and BT-7s would also see combat against the Japanese army in the Far East between 1938 and 1939. It was during these clashes that the vulnerability of the gasoline-engine-powered BT-5 and BT-7 to enemy anti-tank weapons and their propensity to burn when struck caught the attention of the Red Army senior leadership. This no doubt pushed the Red Army's adoption of diesel-powered engines in the BT-7M and other next-generation tanks.

BT-5 and BT-7 tanks would also take part in the Red Army's invasion of Poland

Being shipped by rail is a unit of T-60 tanks with their turrets reversed. By early 1942 it was clear to the Red Army that the vehicle had no significant role on the battlefield as it was both under-gunned and under-armoured. This made it extremely vulnerable to all enemy anti-tank weapons it encountered. (*Bob Fleming*)

The Red Army decided to use the T-60 tank as a base upon which to develop a new up-armoured and up-gunned vehicle designated the T-70 tank, and a further improved version, the T-70M. A running example of a T-70M is seen here at Kubinka with museum staff in period uniforms. (R. Bazalevsky)

in late September 1939 and during the Russo-Finnish War. It was during the Russo-Finnish War that the thin armour protection on the BT-5 and BT-7 again was a serious issue as they proved vulnerable to the entire inventory of enemy anti-tank weapons. Many of the Red Army's BT series tanks were lost in the first few months of combat following the German invasion of the Soviet Union, although enough BTs survived in the Far East for them to take part in the invasion of Manchuria in 1945.

Armament on the T-70 series consisted of a 45mm main gun and a coaxial 7.62mm machine gun. The T-70M carried seventy main gun rounds. Front hull armour on the T-70 series was 45mm thick with hull sides of the same thickness. Pictured is a T-70M in an ambush position. (*Bob Fleming*)

A T-70 tank carrying infantry is seen passing a destroyed German Panzer IV medium tank. The tank was powered by two gasoline engines on either side of the hull coupled together and in the T-70M the engines were placed one behind the other. The vehicle was 14ft (4.27m) long, 7ft 7in (2.3m) wide and had a height of 6ft 8in (2.03m). (*Bob Fleming*)

On display at Kubinka is a T-70 tank. It has a simple visor slit for the driver, in contrast to the T-70M that had a rotating periscope located at the top of the driver's hatch. The problems with the T-70 series included the one-man turret crew and its thin armour. (*Vladimir Yakubov*)

Unhappiness with the T-70 series led the Red Army to request a new light tank with thicker armour and with a two-man turret crew. That tank was designated the T-80 and is seen here on display at Kubinka. It did not impress anybody and only seventy-five were built. (*Vladimir Yakubov*)

Another British tank acquired in 1930 by the Red Army for evaluation was the twin-turreted machine-gun-armed Vickers Mark E. The Red Army was impressed with the vehicle's design and ordered a slightly different version of it into production as the three-man T-26 Model 1931 seen in this photograph. *(Bob Fleming)*

The only surviving example of the T-26 Model 1931 resides at the Central Armed Forces Museum in Moscow, Russia. Each of the vehicle's two one-man turrets was armed with a single 7.62mm machine gun. The vehicle was 16ft 1in (4.9m) long, 11ft 2in (3.4m) wide and had a height of 7ft 9in (2.36m). *(Vladimir Yakubov)*

Believing that the T-26 Model 1931 was insufficiently armed, it was decided that a portion of the production run of the vehicle would have their right side turret armed with a short barrel 37mm gun, as seen here with this vehicle on display at Kubinka. (*Vladimir Yakubov*)

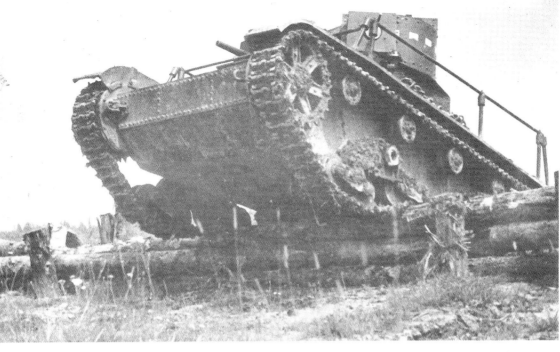

The majority of T-26 Model 1931 tanks armed with the short barrel 37mm gun were configured as radio-equipped command tanks designated as the T-26RT. Such a vehicle is seen here with a metal frame antenna surrounding its hull and is pictured crossing a tank obstacle made out of logs. (*Bob Fleming*)

Eventually a new two-man turret was designed to be mounted on the T-26 Model 1931 hull armed with a 45mm main gun. That re-designed and up-gunned vehicle was designated the T-26 Model 1933 and an example in Finnish army markings is seen here on display at the Tank Museum located in Bovington, England. (*Tank Museum*)

It was initially planned by the Red Army that its entire inventory of T-26 Model 1933 light tanks would be equipped with radios. Shortages in production made this impossible, so only command tanks designated the T-26RT Model 1933 seen here prior to a parade had the horseshoe-shaped metal frame antennas fitted. (*Bob Fleming*)

The crewmen of a T-26RT Model 1933 command tank are shown in front of their vehicle. The picture provides a close-up look at the uniforms and accessories worn by Red Army tankers. The vehicle commander on the right holds the signal flags he would employ to direct the non-radio-equipped tanks in his unit. (*Bob Fleming*)

A dramatic picture of a T-26RT Model 1933 command tank exiting a shallow body of water, no doubt during some type of public demonstration, judging by the number of people in the background. Production of the two-man turret armed with a 45mm main gun for the T-26 series began in 1932. (*Bob Fleming*)

A cheerful young Red Army officer stands in front of his radio-equipped T-26RT Model 1933 command tank during a pre-Second World War photo session. Eventually the T-26 series tanks would be fitted with an interphone system to assist the crew in communicating with each other. (*Bob Fleming*)

Crossing a snow bank is a T-26 Model 1933. It would prove to be the most numerous tank in the Red Army inventory before the German invasion of the Soviet Union in June 1941 and easy prey for German medium tanks. (*Bob Fleming*)

Stopped in front of a farmhouse to speak to one of the local inhabitants is the crew of a T-26RT Model 1933 command tank. Secrecy was an important element of the Red Army in the Second World War and only officers had access to maps and the training needed to read them. (*Bob Fleming*)

Soviet heavy industry mastered the art of electric arc-welding in 1935 and applied that newly-acquired skill to the T-26 series of tanks. An example of that construction method is seen here on the turret of this knocked-out vehicle that was designated the T-26 Model 1938. Notice the sloping sides of this new turret design. (*Patton Museum*)

Soviet industry eventually began constructing both the turrets and hulls of the T-26 series tanks using a combination of electric arc-welding and riveting. This method of building tanks is evident in the sloping hull sides of the vehicle pictured. The gun shield is of welded armour construction. (*Bob Fleming*)

Lined up for a parade is a unit of T-26 Model 1938 tanks with those in front being command vehicles with the horseshoe-shaped metal frame antennas. The hulls of the vehicles pictured were still being built using riveting. Notice the headlights attached to the 45mm main gun and the 7.62mm anti-aircraft machine gun. (*Bob Fleming*)

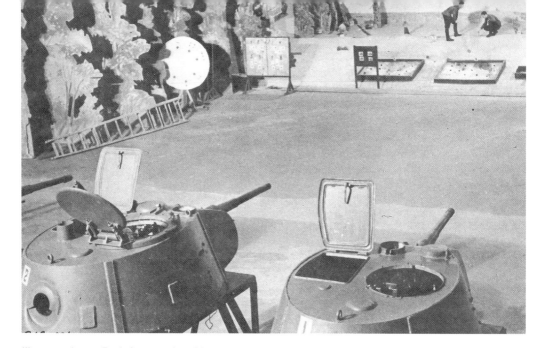

Illustrated is a Red Army sub-calibre training range with the turrets of the T-26 Model 1938 pictured. Notice the opening in the rear of one of the turrets. It was for the fitting of a ball-mounted 7.62mm machine gun. This was a design feature that would appear on many Red Army tanks. (*Bob Fleming*)

On display at Kubinka is a T-26 Model 1940. The gun shield on the vehicle is a casting, instead of welded construction. In spite of the use of sloped armour on the turret and hull of the late production T-26 series tanks, combat experience showed the vehicle remained insufficiently armoured to perform its duties. (*Vladimir Yakubov*)

The most numerous specialized variant of the T-26 series of light tanks constructed were various versions of a flame-thrower tank. The version pictured was designated the KhT-26 or XT-26 and based on the T-26 Model 1931 tank. The two original turrets were replaced with a single turret armed with a flame gun. (*Bob Fleming*)

Based on the T-26 Model 1933 tank was a second-generation flame-thrower version seen here designated the KhT-130. Rather than a specialized turret as was seen on the KhT-26, the original turret was retained and in place of the 45mm main gun was a flame gun. (*Bob Fleming*)

The call for a new light tank arose in 1938 and by 1939 design work had begun on a planned replacement for the T-26 series tank. Pictured on display is an early example of that effort designated the T-126P that never entered production. (*Vladimir Yakubov*)

Sitting on outside display at Kubinka is this production T-50 tank. It retained the 45mm main gun of the T-26 series, but featured a newly-designed turret and hull that took advantage of the additional ballistic protection offered by sloped armour. The armour was also thicker on the T-50 tank than on the T-26 series. (*Vladimir Yakubov*)

On display at the Armoured Vehicle Museum located in Parola, Finland is this T-50 tank captured by the Finnish army from the Red Army during the Second World War. The cupola on the top of the vehicle's turret was for vision ports only and had an opening for signal flags. (*Bob Fleming*)

The Red Army became enthralled with a series of full-tracked armoured vehicles designed by American inventor J. Walter Christie in the 1930s. This was because they could operate with or without their tracks at high speeds for the time. Pictured is one of Christie's vehicles designated the T1 or T3 by the United States army, depending on armament fitted. The United States army tested and eventually rejected the vehicle. (*Patton Museum*)

A side view of a Christie T1/T3 with its tracks on. When removed, the vehicle tracks could be stored on the fenders above the large rubber-rimmed road wheels. Such was the enthusiasm for the Christie-designed full-tracked armoured vehicles that the Red Army acquired two turretless examples in 1931 through an illegal deal with the inventor. (*Patton Museum*)

Once the turretless examples of the Christie armoured vehicles arrived in the Soviet Union, they were quickly copied and designated the BT-2. The locally-designed turret was armed with a 37mm main gun and a 7.62mm machine gun. Key distinguishing features of the BT-2 were the sloping front turret roof and the glacis coming to a flat point. (*Steve Zaloga*)

There was also a version of the BT-2 that was armed with three turret-mounted 7.62mm machine guns; two in place of the 37mm main gun and another in a ball mount on the right side of the vehicle's turret. Pictured is a knocked-out and burning machine-gun-armed only model of the BT-2. (*Patton Museum*)

As the 37mm main gun on the BT-2 was considered inadequate, the vehicle was quickly fitted with a new turret with a flat roof plate as seen here and armed with a 45mm main gun and a coaxial 7.62mm machine gun. In this configuration the vehicle was designated the BT-5, or in this case a BT-5RT. The tank was 18ft 4in (5.58m) long, 7ft 4in (2.23m) wide and 7ft 5in (2.26m) tall. (*Bob Fleming*)

A BT-5RT is shown in this dramatically-composed photograph during a training manoeuvre with two Red Army infantrymen posed in the foreground. Unlike the BT-2 the BT-5 had a rear turret bustle. (*Bob Fleming*)

On display at Kubinka is this BT-5 in the wheels-only running configuration. A portion of the vehicle's track is stored on top of the fender. A distinguishing feature of the BT-2 and BT-5 was the driver's hatch that projected out from the vehicle's glacis plate. (*Vladimir Yakubov*)

The driver of a BT-5RT poses for the photographer. He entered and left the vehicle through a two-piece hinged hatch arrangement seen here with the upper hatch containing his direct-view vision block. This was the same arrangement on the BT-2. (*Bob Fleming*)

A large number of BT-5 tanks pass by the photographer during a pre-Second World War parade. The vehicle was powered by a 400hp gasoline engine that gave a maximum speed on level ground of 45 mph (72 kph). On the road the vehicle had an operational range of 124 miles (200km) and 55 miles (88km) off-road. (*Bob Fleming*)

The BT-5 would see action during the Spanish Civil War (1936–39) and the Soviet invasion of Finland (1939–40). The greatest loss of BT-5s occurred with the German invasion of the Soviet Union in 1941. Here we see German soldiers removing the dead crewmen of a Red Army BT-5. (*Patton Museum*)

The BT-5 follow-on was the BT-7 Model 1935 seen here on display at the Central Armed Forces Museum in Moscow, Russia. Identifying features of the BT-7 included the incorporation of the projected driver hatch (seen on the BT-2 and BT-5) into the front hull plate of the vehicle and the rounded front lower hull. (*Vladimir Yakubov*)

Clearly visible on this abandoned or knocked-out BT-7RT Model 1935 is the pronounced rear turret bustle that first appeared on the BT-5. Also visible are the large armoured hinges for the driver's two-piece fold-out hatches. (*Patton Museum*)

The BT-7 soon sported an improved turret design seen here that did away with that inherited from the BT-5. The new turret came with sloping sides and was constructed from welding and some riveting, as was the vehicle's hull. (*Patton Museum*)

Driving up a snow bank is a BT-7 Model 1937. Power for the vehicle came from a 500hp gasoline engine that provided it with a maximum road speed of 53 mph (85 kph). Besides a more powerful engine than the BT-5, the BT-7 Model 1937 had an improved transmission and suspension system. (*Bob Fleming*)

Visible are two parked BT-7 Model 1937 tanks. Notice that the mufflers are enclosed which was not the case with the BT-5 series. The first combat for the BT-7 occurred in August 1939 against the Japanese army. (*Charles Kliment*)

This photograph of the three-man crew of a BT-7 Model 1937 tank looking over a map allows for a close-up view of the turret and gun shield. Notice one of the two brackets attached to the rear of the main gun for the mounting of a pair of headlights for night-firing, a feature discontinued in 1938. (*Bob Fleming*)

BT-7 Model 1937 tanks are pictured during a pre-Second World War parade. The vehicle was 18ft 6in (5.63m) long, 7ft 6in (2.28m) wide and 7ft 11in (2.41m) tall. Armour on the vehicle was a maximum of 20mm thick on later production units. The BT-7 Model 1937 had storage space for 146 main gun rounds. (*Patton Museum*)

The final version of the BT-7 series of tanks was fitted with a more fuel-efficient diesel engine. With this change the vehicle was designated the BT-7M or the BT-8. The only outward distinguishing feature of the BT-7M/BT-8 was a rear turret-mounted machine gun as seen on the vehicle in the middle of the picture. (*Patton Museum*)

Chapter Two

Medium Tanks

The first medium tanks in Red Army service were captured examples of the British-designed and built Mark A 'Whippet' that came from the White Army inventory. This vehicle had first appeared in British army service in early 1918 and was intended for exploitation purposes, pushing behind enemy lines, attacking artillery positions and command posts. The 31,360-lb (14.225mt) vehicle had a three-man crew and was armed with four 7.7mm machine guns. Maximum armour thickness on the Whippet's front hull was 14mm.

In Red Army service the Whippet was known as the *Tyeilor* after the two Taylor gasoline engines that powered the vehicle. The Whippets would last in

The first medium tanks in the Red Army inventory were captured examples of the British-designed and built Mark A Whippet. The vehicle was armed only with machine guns. This particular example of the Whippet belongs to the United States Army Ordnance Museum collection. (*Michael Green*)

Exiting a building during a public ceremony in Russia during their Civil War (1917–22) is a Mark A Whippet medium tank. British tankers had arrived with the Whippets to teach the anti-Bolshevik White Army how to operate the vehicle. This training process met with little success. (*Tank Museum*)

Red Army service until a shortage of spare parts rendered them immobile by the early 1920s.

A medium tank acquired by the Red Army in the 1930s for consideration and testing was the British-designed and built Mark II medium tank. This 30,128-lb (13.666mt) vehicle had entered British army service in 1926 and was protected by a maximum armour thickness of 12mm on the front of its turret. With a five-man crew, the Mark II was armed with a turret-mounted 47mm main gun and three 7.7mm machine guns. The Red Army was not impressed with the Mark II and never sought to copy it.

In what turned out to be a design dead end, the Red Army had looked at an up-scaled T-18 light tank that could fulfil the role of medium tank. That vehicle was designated the T-12 medium tank and it was originally conceived that thirty would be built. Sadly, the design proved badly flawed and only one was built. In its place an improved version designated the T-24 medium tank was approved. A prototype of the vehicle appeared in 1931 with twenty-four additional units built shortly thereafter, eventually armed with a 45mm main gun. In service the T-24 proved a disappointment and was soon employed strictly for training duties.

Likely inspired by multi-turreted British tank prototypes built in the late 1920s, the Red Army began developmental work on its first indigenous-built medium tank. The fruits of that labour eventually appeared in prototype form in 1932, with the first production units of a multi-turreted vehicle rolling off the factory floor in 1933 with the designation T-28 Model 1934 Medium Tank. The gasoline-engine-powered vehicle had a crew of six men who were protected by a maximum armour thickness of 30mm on the front of the turret.

The armament of the 61,728-lb (28mt) T-28 Model 1934 Medium Tank was located in three different turrets. The uppermost turret had 360 degrees of traverse and was armed with a short-barrelled 76.2mm main gun. Instead of a coaxial machine gun, the right front of the turret featured a ball-mounted 7.62mm machine gun. The turret was almost identical to the one mounted on the Red Army T-35 heavy tank series.

Among the British-designed and built tanks acquired by the Red Army in the 1930s for technical evaluation was the Mark II medium tank seen here belonging to the Tank Museum at Bovington, England. (*Tank Museum*)

At the Central Armed Forces Museum in Moscow, Russia is a T-28 medium tank accepted into Red Army service in 1933. It was fitted with three turrets: a large upper turret armed with a 76.2mm main gun that traversed 360 degrees, and two lower 7.62mm machine-gun-armed sub-turrets with much more limited traverse. (*Vladimir Yakubov*)

Located in the front hull and below the main turret of the T-28 were two small one-man sub-turrets with limited traverse, each armed with a single 7.62mm machine gun. These sub-turrets were also copied from the ones used on the T-35 heavy tank series. With the introduction of a modernized version of the vehicle, designated T-28 Model 1938 Medium Tank, the 76.2mm main gun was replaced by a longer-barrelled 76.2mm gun that offered superior armour penetration abilities. Some T-28s had additional machine guns mounted in the rear and top of the turret, bringing the total armament up to one 76.2mm cannon and five machine guns.

From 1934 until 1940 there were 503 units built of the T-28 series. They would first see service during the Red Army invasion of Poland. Combat experience gained in the Russo-Finnish War quickly highlighted the fact that the vehicle was under-armoured which resulted in a number of the T-28 tanks having applique armour added. The add-on armour boosted the maximum armour thickness of the tank to 80mm and pushed the vehicle's weight up to 70,547lb (32mt). The last twelve units of the T-28 series were designated the

This German wartime picture of a captured Red Army T-28 medium tank lists the thickness of the vehicle's armour at various locations on both the hull and turrets. Between the two sub-turrets is the driver's position with his hatch in the open position. (*Patton Museum*)

On display at the Armoured Vehicle Museum at Parola, Finland is this Red Army T-28 medium tank captured by the Finnish army during the Russo-Finnish War which lasted from 1939 until 1940. Combat experience gained during the conflict resulted in the vehicle being up-armoured. (*Andreas Kirchhoff*)

T-28 Medium Tank 1940 and featured the same turrets with sloped armour fitted to the last production run of the T-35 heavy tank series.

Those T-28 series tanks that survived the Russo-Finnish War would face the German army in the summer of 1941. The majority of the T-28 series tanks were quickly lost to non-combat causes such as mechanical failure or lack of fuel. A few survived to see service during the defence of Moscow and Leningrad until the end of the blockade in 1944.

Always attempting to improve its tank inventory, the Red Army had instigated the development of a possible replacement medium tank for the T-28 series. The only vehicle that showed any promise at that time was a 39,682-lb (18mt) medium tank design designated the A-20 that was intended as a replacement for the BT series. Work on the A-20 was initiated in November 1937. The main gun on the proposed A-20 was to be the same 45mm main gun mounted in the BT-5 and BT-7. Maximum armour thickness on the A-20 was to be 22mm on the front of the turret.

The A-20 design featured two big innovations for the Red Army's tank inventory. The first was its use of highly-sloped armour on its hull and turret that greatly improved the vehicle's ability to resist a wide range of battlefield projec-

A motorcycle messenger is pictured delivering orders to the commander of a T-28 medium tank during a pre-Second World War training manoeuvre. Instead of a coaxial machine gun mounted alongside the vehicle's main gun, there was a separate ball mount for a 7.62mm machine gun fitted on the right side of the tank turret as shown. (*Patton Museum*)

tiles. The second was its planned use of a newly-developed diesel-powered engine, referred to as the V-2. The new 12-cylinder engine would increase the vehicle's operational range and also make it far less vulnerable to enemy anti-tank weapons. The first V-2 engine came off the production line in September 1939 and was originally used in the BT-7M.

By the summer of 1938 it was determined that the proposed A-20 might be insufficiently armed and armoured for the medium tank role. The Red Army therefore decided it would need another proposed medium tank design that would be designated the A-32 and have a maximum armour thickness on the front of the turret of 32mm. It would be armed with a short-barrelled 76.2mm main gun.

By May 1939 it was decided to thicken the maximum armour on the front of the A-32 turret to 45mm. This up-armoured version of the vehicle was designated the A-34 in the summer of 1939. In August 1939 the Red Army decided to adopt the A-34; a decision concurred with by Joseph Stalin, the leader of the Soviet Union, in December 1939. The first A-34 prototype appeared in January

Looking into the turret of a six-man T-28 medium tank, the breech of the vehicle's 76.2mm main gun is visible. The T-28 was 24ft 5in (7.44m) long, had a width of 9ft 5in (2.87m), was 9ft 3in (2.81m) tall and had a maximum operational range of 135 miles (217km) on level roads. (*Bob Fleming*)

1940, with the second prototype rolling off the factory floor the following month.

To prove the reliability of the A-34 prototype tanks before submitting them for the final approval of the Red Army, a demonstration run that would encompass a distance of 1,800 miles (2,897km) during the winter months of February and March 1940 was arranged. On 17 March 1940, the two A-34 prototypes arrived in Moscow for a personal inspection by Stalin and other high-ranking members of the government and military élite. Despite the misgivings by some that the A-34 was not yet suitable for production, Stalin gave his blessing to the production of the vehicle once any design faults uncovered during testing by the Red Army were addressed.

Additional testing of the A-34 prototypes led to the conclusion that the vehicle was superior to any other tank then in Red Army service, and by the end of March 1940 the tank was approved for production as the T-34. Besides a short-barrelled 76.2mm main gun, the T-34 would also be armed with a coaxial 7.62mm machine gun and another 7.62mm machine gun in the front hull. The first 150 units of the T-34 also featured a 7.62mm machine gun in a ball mount in the rear of the turret.

Following the T-28 medium tank into service was the innovative four-man T-34 medium tank. The example pictured was designated as the T-34 Model 1940. It was armed with the 76.2mm L-11 main gun and can be readily identified by the oddly-shaped gun shield. The driver's hatch had a single forward-facing periscope. (*Patton Museum*)

Despite production of the four-man T-34 being approved, there were still some hurdles that had to be overcome. One of the original requirements called for the vehicle to operate over 1,864 miles (3,000km) without a major break-down. A mileage test done in April 1940 showed that the tank could not meet this requirement. However, this was soon dropped to 621 miles (1,000km). The Red Army went ahead and placed an order with two factories for 600 T-34s to be built starting in June 1940. They also placed a production order for 2,800 units of the T-34 for 1941.

Some within the Red Army who opposed the production of the T-34 proposed an upgraded version, designated the T-34M. Among its many features it would have a larger three-man turret, allowing the vehicle commander to concentrate on directing his crew rather than doing double duty as the tank's gunner as was the arrangement in the T-34. In addition, the Christie suspension system would be replaced on the T-34M with a torsion bar version. With these improvements, plans were put forward to replace the T-34 on the production lines with the T-34M in the autumn of 1941. The German invasion of the Soviet Union in the summer of 1941 quickly resulted in this project being terminated as the Red Army could ill afford any disruption in the production of the T-34 for fear it could not replace its battlefield losses.

The first production unit of the Red Army's new 58,912-lb (29mt) medium tank rolled off the production line in September 1940. This vehicle is now commonly referred to as the T-34 Model 1940. By the time the German army invaded the Soviet Union in June 1941, 1,225 units of the T-34 Model 1940 were in service, of which 967 had been delivered to field units. Maximum armour thickness on the front of the vehicle's turret was 45mm.

Initial German army encounters with the T-34 Model 1940 raised a great deal of alarm among both their infantry and armour branches. Their existing anti-tank weapons proved unable to penetrate the thick, well-sloped armour on the T-34, and the vehicle's 76.2mm main gun easily penetrated the armour on the German Panzer III and Panzer IV medium tanks it encountered. This would eventually lead to the up-gunning and up-armouring of the existing German medium tanks, and the development of the German Panther medium tank series and Tiger E heavy tank as a counter to the T-34.

This early T-34 Model 1940 tank can be identified by the twin front hull headlights and the bottom of the glacis plate bolted to the lower front hull plate. It also has two small periscopes just above the driver's hatch facing sideways and early-style tow shackles. (*Patton Museum*)

The follow-on to the T-34 Model 1940 was the T-34 Model 1941 seen here. It was armed with a longer-barrelled 76.2mm main gun designated the F-34. Notice the serrated and pierced rubber-rimmed road wheels that lasted in service till the end of the Second World War. (*Michael Green*)

The Red Army early war battlefield technical superiority in medium tanks was offset by the fact that the T-34 Model 1940 was just entering service and their crews often had little training in the use of their new tanks. Compounding the problem was the fact that most of the tanks did not have radios. There were also shortages of everything from main gun ammunition to fuel and spare parts for the T-34-equipped units confronting the Germans, and these factors allowed their army to easily prevail over the Red Army during the early phase of their invasion of the Soviet Union.

The 76.2mm main gun initially selected for use by the Red Army on the T-34 Model 1940 was designated the L-11. It was not the desired weapon in the opinion of the vehicle's designers due to its relatively low muzzle velocity and hence poor armour penetration ability. Due to almost everybody's unhappiness with the L-11, other weapons were considered for the T-34 Model 1940, including the ZiS-4 57mm anti-tank gun. A few of these were actually mounted in the vehicle to test their effectiveness.

As there was a new 76.2mm main gun with a longer barrel, and hence better

An external feature common to all T-34 series tanks armed with the 76.2mm F-34 main gun was the bolted armoured housing that extended out from the gun shield partially over the rear portion of the weapon's barrel as seen in this picture. Its job was to protect the weapon's hydropneumatic recuperator. (*Chris Hughes*)

armour penetration abilities, being developed for the KV-I heavy tank designated the F-32, work was begun in early 1940 to modify it for mounting in the T-34 Model 1940. The new tank gun was designated the F-34 and had a slightly longer barrel than the F-32. It first appeared on some T-34 Model 1940 tanks in February 1941. Vehicles so equipped were designated the T-34 Model 1941. Due to temporary shortages, some T-34 Model 1941 tanks would be armed with the F-32 76.2mm tank gun in place of the F-34. Maximum armour thickness on the turret front of the T-34 Model 1941 was 52mm.

Additional improvements to the T-34 series resulted in the redesign of some components to increase the vehicle's combat effectiveness. Vehicles so modified were designated the T-34 Model 1942. The maximum armour thickness on the turret front of the vehicle was now 65mm. An internal change was an increase in armour protection on the sides of the T-34 Model 1942 hull from 40mm to 45mm.

The most noticeable external changes to the T-34 Model 1942 were the replacement of the original rectangular transmission access hatch with a new oval hatch, as well as a new driver's hatch with two periscopes instead of the single periscope on earlier vehicles. Some factories building the T-34 series tank would incorporate features of the T-34 Model 1941 and the T-34 Model 1942 on the same vehicle, resulting in the designation T-34 Model 1941/42.

Following the T-34 Model 1942 into production was the T-34 Model 1943. It can be readily identified by its new hexagonal-shaped turret that was borrowed from the never-built T-34M. Maximum armour protection on the turret front of the T-34 Model 1943 was 70mm. Besides the new turret design, the T-34 Model 1943 featured a number of drivetrain improvements.

Despite the new turret on the T-34 Model 1943 being larger and having more

Unlike contemporary tanks of the day that had their transmissions mounted in the front hull, the transmission of the T-34 series tanks was mounted in the rear hull. Early production T-34 series tanks, including the T-34 Model 1941 tank seen here, featured a rectangular transmission access hatch in the rear hull. (*Patton Museum*)

With the introduction of the T-34 Model 1942 tank a number of changes occurred, including the replacement of the original rectangular transmission access hatch in the rear hull with a circular example as pictured here. On either side of the transmission access hatch are the cast homogenous armour (CHA) housings for the exhaust mufflers. (*Patton Museum*)

room than the turrets seen on earlier versions of the T-34 series, the two-man turret crew was retained on this latest model. To improve visibility, the turret was eventually fitted with an overhead cupola for the vehicle commander, which could only have been used when he was not engaged in aiming and firing the tank's main gun.

To improve the operational range of the T-34 Model 1943, a pair of large box-like external fuel tanks were devised that attached to the rear of the vehicle's hull. These first appeared during the summer of 1942. They were later replaced by three large cylindrical external fuel canisters in early 1943, with two located on the right side of the upper rear hull and the other one being located on the left side of the upper hull. The external fuel tanks did not connect to the vehicle's

The power for the entire T-34 series of medium tanks was a very compact, water-cooled V-12 four-stroke diesel engine with twelve cylinders arranged at an angle of 60 degrees in two banks. The engine produced 500hp and could propel the vehicle to a maximum road speed of 34 mph (55 kph). (*Vladimir Yakubov*)

interior fuel tanks. To move fuel from the external tanks to the vehicle's internal tanks required a fuel pump.

By the time production of the T-34 Model 1943 ended in 1944, approximately 35,000 units had been built of the T-34 series armed with the 76.2mm main gun.

In January 1943 the Red Army began looking at the concept of a universal tank that could replace the existing T-34 series and the KV-1 series heavy tanks. One of the prototype vehicles was designated the T-43; another one was KV-13, a smaller lighter version of the KV-1S heavy tank. It would be similar to the cancelled T-34M project as it was envisioned that it would have a new three-man turret (retaining the F-34 76.2mm main gun) and run on a torsion bar suspension system. It differed from the proposed T-34M due to its increased emphasis

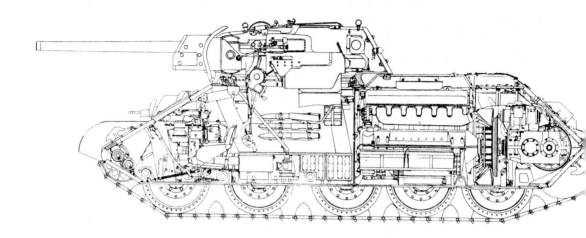

This illustration shows the arrangement of the engine and the transmission in an early production T-34 series tank. Placing the transmission in the rear hull of the vehicle meant there was no drive train bisecting the lower hull as there was with tanks having a front-hull-mounted transmission, allowing the designers to lower the height of the T-34 tank compared to its western counterparts. (*Patton Museum*)

on armour protection, with a maximum armour on the turret front of 90mm compared to 70mm on the turret front of the T-34M.

Testing in March 1943 of the T-43 showed that the extra weight of the increased armour protection greatly reduced its battlefield mobility compared to the T-34 series. The summer battles of 1943 highlighted the fact that it was not the armour protection levels of the T-34 series they needed to worry about as much as having a tank that mounted a main gun able to penetrate the armour of the German Panther medium tank and the Tiger E heavy tank. This realization pushed the Red Army to look for a larger, more powerful main gun for the T-34 series and cancel work on the T-43, whose introduction would have disrupted T-34 production.

The first appearance of the Tiger E heavy tank on the Eastern Front in August 1942 had made the Red Army aware of the fact that it needed to up-gun the T-34 series. In response it had tasked several design bureaus with the development of a suitable 85mm tank gun. However, as the number of German heavy tanks being encountered was low, the development of the 85mm gun languished. The many large tank battles of the summer of 1943 that saw the fielding and increasing number of German heavy tanks and the new Panther medium tank had quickly added a renewed sense of urgency to the development and fielding of an 85mm tank gun by the Red Army.

In spite of the fact that the design for the final version of a suitable 85mm tank

A key identifying feature of early production T-34 series tanks was the large one-piece hatch in the turret roof that hinged forward as is seen in this photograph of a crew cleaning the barrel of their main gun. The reason for this awkward arrangement is lost to history as it obstructed the forward vision of the vehicle commander when in the open position. (*Patton Museum*)

gun and the vehicle itself were not yet finalized, Red Army testing of two 85mm gun-armed prototypes went so well that the vehicle was approved by Stalin and the Red Army for production as the T-34-85. Stalin wanted the tank in production by February 1944. The 85mm main gun finally selected for mounting in the T-34-85 was designated the ZiS-S-53. The tanks that were fitted with this new 85mm gun are now commonly referred to as the T-34-85 Model 1944. Due to delays in production of the ZiS-S-53 gun, the first 800 or so units were fitted with another 85mm main gun designated the D-5T and are sometimes called the T-34-85 Model 1943.

Maximum armour thickness on the front of the T-34-85 turret was 90mm. The thicker armour on the T-34-85 series and the larger turret brought the weight of the vehicle up to 70,547lb (32mt). This weight gain resulted in some minor loss in battlefield mobility for the T-34-85 compared to the original T-34 tank armed with the 76.2mm main gun.

The first T-34-85s began arriving in field units in March 1944, with élite armoured units getting priority on delivery. The arrival of the vehicle was a great morale-booster to Red Army tankers who had been fighting at a great disadvantage when dealing with late-war German tanks with the 76.2mm main gun on the T-34. The 85mm main gun on the T-34-85 imparted a degree of parity in fighting effectiveness between the two opponents' tank units.

Total T-34-85 production between 1943 and 1945 was in the order of 23,000 units. Production of the vehicle would be continued in the Soviet Union after the Second World War with both the wartime production and post-war production

Located at Kubinka is this early production T-34 Model 1941 with twin headlights, a bolted glacis and an early-style driver's hatch with a single forward-facing periscope. The majority of early production T-34 series tanks had a welded armour turret, as does this vehicle. (*Vladimir Yakubov*)

vehicles going through two modernization programmes, one in 1960 and the second in 1969. Both Poland and Czechoslovakia received permission to build licence-produced versions of the T-34-85 beginning in the early 1950s, many of which were exported around the world to serve in a large number of foreign armies.

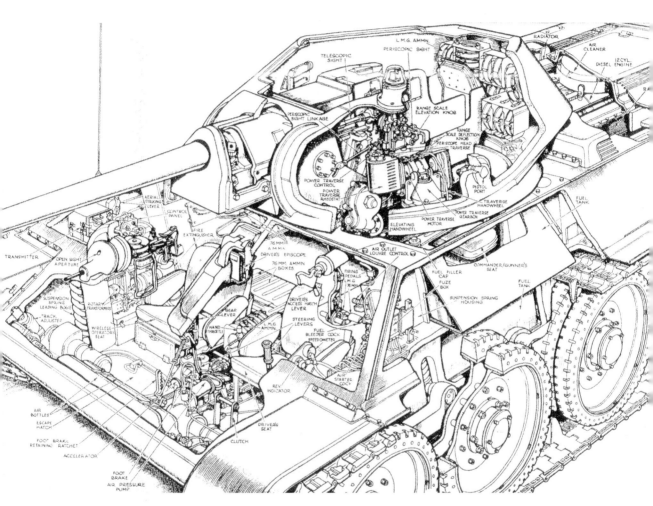

From a British army technical evaluation report done on the T-34 Model 1942 tank during the Second World War appears this line illustration identifying many of the vehicle's components and parts. The vehicle was 22ft (6.7m) long, 9ft 6in (2.9m) wide and topped out at 8ft (2.4m) tall. (*Patton Museum*)

Some early production T-34 series tanks had a cast armour turret, as does the T-34 Model 1942 pictured here. The vehicle shown has the later production hammerhead towing shackles. The original twin front-hull-mounted headlights have been replaced by a single headlight on the left-hand side of the vehicle's hull. (*Patton Museum*)

An interesting comparison photograph of a T-34 Model 1942 with a cast armour turret and a United States army M4A4 medium tank also fitted with a cast armour turret. Clearly the Soviet tank would be a much harder target to acquire and hit on the battlefield than the much taller American tank. (*Patton Museum*)

Pictured is a T-34 Model 1942. The external features that mark the vehicle include the new driver's hatch, which now has two forward-facing periscopes with armoured covers instead of the original single forward-facing periscope seen on the T-34 Model 1940 and Model 1941. It also has a new gun shield fitted over the bow machine-gun port. (*Patton Museum*)

To build as many T-34 series tanks as quickly as possible, there was an interim version of the vehicle produced by the Stalingrad Tractor Plant designated the T-34 Model 41/42. An example is pictured here being examined by German soldiers. Distinguishing features of this vehicle are the chisel-shaped hydro-pneumatic recuperator housing and the all-steel road wheels. (*Patton Museum*)

This picture shows the twin hatches that appeared on the T-34 Model 1943 tank. These new hatches are also hinged to open forward instead of rearward as on western tanks. Notice the large mushroom-shaped armoured housing on the rear of the turret containing the upper portion of the electrically-operated ventilating blower. (*Chris Hughes*)

There was a great deal of unhappiness with the awkward single-piece hatch cover on early production T-34 series tanks. This led to the development of the T-34 Model 1943 seen here with separate overhead hatches for the loader and the vehicle commander/gunner and a new, roomier hexagonal-shaped turret. (*Patton Museum*)

A knocked-out T-34 Model 1943 lies halfway in a large shell-hole that is being occupied by a German army 81mm mortar team. The white marking on the turret roof is for aircraft recognition purposes to prevent fratricide. (*Patton Museum*)

Two T-34 Model 1943 tanks rush into battle. The vehicle in the foreground is fitted with box-shaped external fuel carriers on the rear hull. These came in two different versions with both eventually being replaced by three rounded fuel drums, one on the left rear hull side and two on the right rear hull side. (*Patton Museum*)

Pictured is this restored T-34 Model 1943 tank. Unlike earlier versions of the T-34 series that predominantly had welded armour turrets, the majority of turrets for the T-34 Model 1943 tank were made from cast armour. One of the three cylindrical fuel canisters fitted to this first-generation T-34 series tank can be seen on the rear of this vehicle's hull. (*Michael Green*)

From the turret bustle looking forward inside a T-34 Model 1942 tank can be seen the breech end of the 76.2mm F-34 main gun along with the vehicle commander/gunner's controls. The optical gun sights on Red Army tanks were of much poorer quality than those found on their German counterparts. (*Patton Museum*)

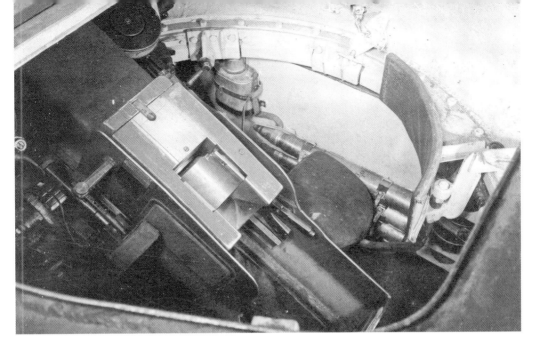

Looking into the turret of a T-34 Model 1942 tank from the left-hand side of the vehicle one can see the loader's seat and backrest on the right as well as some ready rounds stored along the side of the hull. Extending from the rear of the breech is the recoil guard that doubled as a catch basin for the spent main gun cartridge cases. (*Patton Museum*)

Visible from the driver's seat looking rearward into the hull of a T-34 Model 1942 tank is the vehicle commander/gunner's seat on the right-hand side of the picture. The loader's seat is seen on the left-hand side of the photograph. Unlike its German medium tank counterparts, the T-34 series did not have a turret basket. (*Patton Museum*)

The main gun ready rounds for T-34 series tanks were stored on the inside walls of the turret as seen in this interior picture of a T-34 Model 1942. The bulk of the main gun rounds were stored in metal boxes visible on the hull floor of the vehicle that were covered with rubber mats when not being accessed by the loader. (*Patton Museum*)

Looking into the turret of a T-34 Model 1943 tank one can see the recoil guard for the 76.2mm main gun and the racks for the spare drum magazines for the 7.62mm machine guns mounted on the vehicle. (*Chris Hughes*)

From under the breech ring of a T-34 Model 1943 tank's main gun looking forward, the driver's seat is visible on the left and the radioman/machine-gunner's seat on the right. Also visible are the vehicle's radio on the right-hand side of the picture and the driver's instrument panel on the left. (*Chris Hughes*)

Pictured is a knocked-out T-34 Model 1943 tank that has suffered a catastrophic main gun ammu-nition explosion which has forced the vehicle's turret off the hull. The bottle-shaped object protruding from the front of the vehicle's turret roof is the armoured housing for the vehicle commander/gunner's overhead panoramic periscope sight. (*Patton Museum*)

Littering a battlefield is this knocked-out T-34 Model 1943 tank. Unlike the majority of T-34 Model 1943 tanks that had a cast armour hexagonal-shaped turret, this vehicle's turret was made with a large hydraulic press whose use can be identified by the upper rounded edges of the turret. (*Patton Museum*)

Pictured at a Soviet factory is a line of T-34 Model 1943 tanks on the assembly line. The ability of Soviet industry to churn out thousands upon thousands of the T-34 series during the Second World War made up for their high battlefield losses. In 1942 the Red Army lost about 15,000 tanks, followed by approximately 22,400 more in 1943. (*Patton Museum*)

No doubt influenced by the vehicle commander cupolas seen on German medium tanks, the Red Army eventually adopted a similar component for their late production T-34 Model 1943 tanks as seen on this example on display at the Armoured Vehicle Museum at Parola, Finland. (*Andreas Kirchhoff*)

A line of captured T-34 Model 1943 tanks with the late production vehicle commander's cupola are seen here with the German unit who captured them proudly announcing that fact with a hand-made sign on the vehicle in the foreground. Some German units – up to battalion size – would employ captured T-34 series tanks during the fighting on the Eastern Front. (*Patton Museum*)

Combat experience in the summer of 1943 demonstrated to the Red Army that the 76.2mm main gun on the first generation of T-34 series tanks was obsolete. To rectify the situation, the Red Army fielded a second-generation version of the vehicle referred to as the T-34-85 Model 1943. A number are seen here during a handing-over ceremony in March 1944. (*Bob Fleming*)

These early production T-34-85 Model 1943 tanks are armed with the D-5T 85mm main gun that can be identified by the distinctive thick circular bolted collar covering a portion of the gun where it protrudes out of its shield. This version of the T-34-85 series also featured the rounded front fenders inherited from the T-34 Model 1943 and a radio antenna in the right front hull. (*Patton Museum*)

Pictured is one of the first production units of the T-34-85 Model 1944 armed with the improved ZiS-S-53 85mm main gun. It can be identified by a new type of armoured collar covering a portion of the gun where it protrudes out of the shield. The T-34-85 Model 1944 retained rounded front fenders. (*Patton Museum*)

The turret on this destroyed T-34-85 tank has the inverted U-shaped turret-lifting hooks that identify it as a T-34-85 Model 1943 or an early production T-34-85 Model 1944 tank. As it lacks a radio antenna mount on the forward portion of the right hull it can be identified as a Model 1944 as the radio was moved inside the vehicle's turret and the whip antenna relocated to the turret roof. (*Bob Fleming*)

A column of Red Army T-34-85 tanks moves through a damaged Eastern European city on the way to Berlin, the capital of Nazi Germany. The vehicle in the foreground can be identified as a T-34-85 Model 1944 tank by the rounded front fenders and the roof-mounted radio antenna that is hard to see in this photograph. (*Patton Museum*)

This picture shows a T-34-85 Model 1944 turret mounted on a rebuilt T-34 Model 1943 hull. The T-34 Model 1943 front lower hull can be identified by the section where the lower portion of the glacis plate joins with the rounded front portion of the hull floor plate. The turrets on the T-34-85 Model 1943 and Model 1944 could only be traversed manually. (*Bob Fleming*)

On display at Kubinka is this T-34-85 armed with a ZiS-S-53 85mm main gun. The vehicle can be identified as a T-34-85 Model 1945 by its squared front fenders. The standard production T-34-85 series tank glacis plate formed a sharp angle where it was welded to the lower front hull plate. (*Vladimir Yakubov*)

This overhead view shows the turret roof of a T-34-85 tank. It can be identified as a Model 1945 by the one-piece vehicle commander's hatch and the rectangular bulge on the lower left-hand side of the turret that marks it as a vehicle with an electric turret-traversing system. The T-34-85 was 8ft 6in (2.59m) tall. (*Chris Hughes*)

Visible on this example of a T-34-85 Model 1945 are the squared fenders and the antenna mount on the left-hand side of the turret roof. This vehicle also features cast rubber-rimmed spoked road wheels constructed during the Second World War alongside the more common concave road wheels. (*Andreas Kirchoff*)

The rear vehicle in this column of tanks is a T-34-85 Model 1944. It has the original two-piece vehicle commander's split overhead hatch that was replaced on the T-34-85 Model 1945 with a one-piece overhead version. The metal brackets located just above the rear fenders are for holding cylindrical TDP smoke canisters that are missing from the vehicle pictured. (*Bob Fleming*)

Two T-34-85 tanks, either Model 1944 or Model 1945, are seen in this picture with their crews and friends posing for the photographer. The main gun on the T-34-85 tank with its standard BR-365 AP round could deal with the majority of German medium tanks, self-propelled guns and tank destroyers it encountered in 1944 and 1945. (*Bob Fleming*)

A line-up of main gun rounds for the T-34-85 tank. On the far left is the standard high-explosive (HE) round designated the O-365 employed against non-armoured targets. The centre round is the standard BR-365 armour-piercing (AP) and the round on the far right is the far less common BR-365P AP round, the suffix 'P' standing for sub-calibre. (*Patton Museum*)

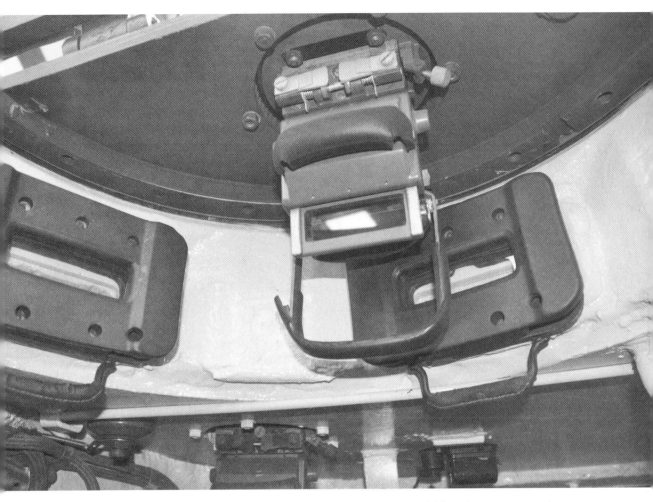

Looking up from the vehicle commander's seat in a T-34-85 Model 1945 tank one can see the cupola with the one-piece overhead hatch. Mounted in the forward portion of the vehicle commander's hatch is a 360-degree traversable periscope. Also visible are some of the vehicle commander's vision blocks with rubber padding around them. (*Chris Hughes*)

A distinctive external feature found on T-34-85 tanks built during the Second World War was the two side-by-side mushroom-shaped armoured housings on the rear of the turret. They contained the upper portion of the two electrically-operated ventilating blowers in the rear of the turret bustle. (*Chris Hughes*)

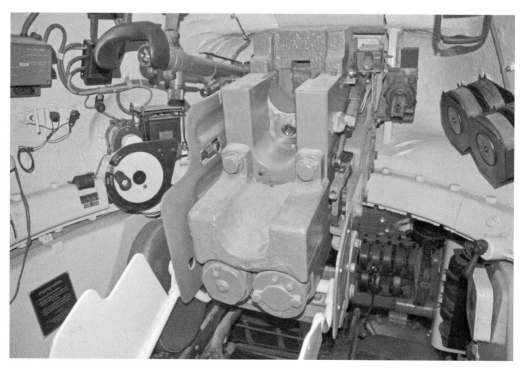

Taken from the loader's left-hand location in a T-34-85 Model 1945 tank is this view of the breech ring and breech block. Just behind and below the breech ring is the recoil guard. Notice the spare drum magazines stored in the upper part of the turret for the 7.62mm machine gun not mounted in this vehicle. (*Chris Hughes*)

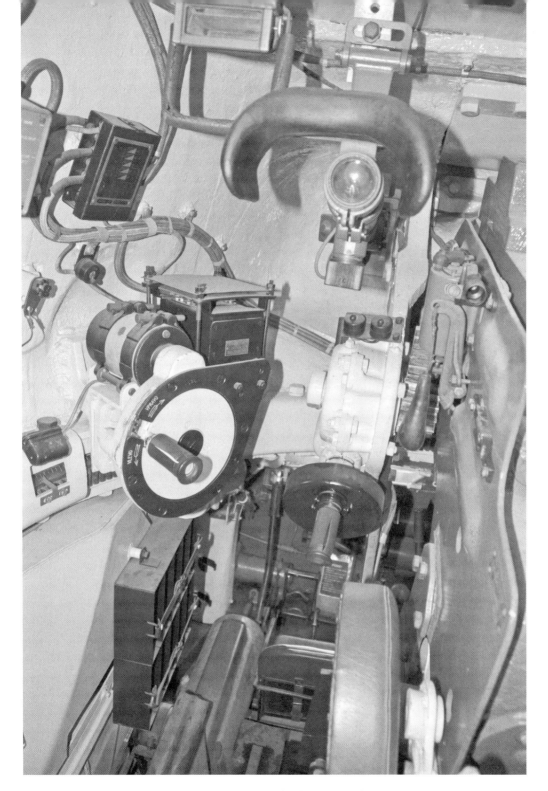

A close-up view of the gunner's position in a T-34-85 Model 1945 tank with the gunner's seat folded up. Visible is the gunner's TSh-16 articulated sighting telescope and his overhead travers-able periscope. The manual turret-traverse handle is on the left of the picture and the elevation handle at the bottom. (*Chris Hughes*)

From the loader's side of this T-34-85 Model 1945 tank is this view of the vehicle commander's radio mounted against the side of the turret wall. To the left of the radio can be seen some of the main gun ammunition racks located in the rear of the vehicle's turret. (*Chris Hughes*)

Taken from under the breech ring of the main gun in a T-34-85 Model 1945 tank is this forward-facing view of the driver/mechanic and machine-gunner's position in the vehicle's front hull. Visible mounted against the lower portion of the front hull are the drum magazines for the on-board machine guns. (*Chris Hughes*)

The T-34-85 pictured is taking part in the annual War and Peace show held in England. The smooth turret casting indicates a Polish or Czech post-war copy of the T-34-85. The tow cable stored on the left hull side of the vehicle just in front on the external fuel canister and the solid rubber road wheels also mark it as a post-war vehicle or rebuilt wartime T-34-85 tank. (*Christophe Vallier*)

Belonging to the collection of the Swiss Tank Museum located at Thun, Switzerland is this post-war Soviet-built T-34-85 Model 1946 tank. The key identifying feature of this vehicle is the relocation of one of the two electrically-operated ventilating blowers from the rear of the turret bustle to the front of the turret roof as seen in this picture. (*Andreas Kirchhoff*)

The planned wartime replacement for the T-34-85 in Red Army service was the T-44 medium tank. This particular vehicle is an upgraded post-war version designated the T-44M. It retained the T-34-85 gun but had a brand-new hull and turret design. Due to serious teething problems the T-44 was not placed into full-scale production during the Second World War. (*Vladimir Yakubov*)

Chapter Three

Heavy Tanks

The first heavy tanks in Red Army service were a small number of British-designed and built Mark V Heavy Tanks captured from the White Army during the Russian Civil War. These vehicles had a crew of eight men and weighed upwards of 64,960lb (29.47mt) depending on their armament. Maximum armour thickness on the vehicle's front hull was 16mm.

In Red Army service the Mark V was referred to as the *Rikardo*, taken from the manufacturer of the gasoline engines that powered the vehicles. These vehicles would last in Red Army service throughout the 1920s. In the Russian language, heavy tank translates as *Tyazholyj Tank*.

Influenced by the multi-turreted British-designed and built Vickers A1E1 Independent heavy tank prototype which weighed 71,680lb (32.51mt) and had an

Belonging to the Tank Museum, Bovington, England is this Mark V heavy tank of First World War vintage. A number of these British-designed and built tanks had been captured by the Red Army during the Russian Civil War and placed back into service against their former owners, the White Army. (*Tank Museum*)

On display at Kubinka is one of the surviving British-designed and built Mark V heavy tanks captured by the Red Army during the Russian Civil War. These vehicles were 26ft 5in (8.05m) long, 13ft 6in (4.11m) wide and had a height of 8ft 8in (2.64m). (*Vladimir Yakubov*)

eight-man crew, the Red Army began design studies for a heavy tank in 1930, which led to the fielding of the eleven-man, gasoline-engine-powered five-turreted T-35 heavy tank series. July of 1932 saw the completion of the first prototype T-35. Construction of the first batch of ten production vehicles would take place between 1933 and 1934.

The standard production version of the T-35 series did not enter service until 1935 with construction continuing until 1938. It was referred to as the T-35 Model 1935 and had a lengthened chassis with four bogie assemblies on either side of the vehicle's hull. This was in contrast to the three bogie assemblies on either side of the first ten units of the T-35 Model 1932 series.

On top of the superstructure of the T-35 Model 1935 was a large 360-degree rotating flat-topped turret shared with the last production batch of T-28 medium

The Red Army drew its inspiration for its first locally-built post-Civil War heavy tank (designated the T-35 series) from a British-designed and built heavy tank named the 'Independent'. The British tank had four machine-gun-armed sub-turrets arrayed around a taller central turret armed with a 47mm main gun as seen here. (*Tank Museum*)

tanks. It was armed with a modified 76.2mm main gun. This was in contrast to the rounded-top 76.2mm gun-armed turret installed on the first ten vehicles. The 76.2mm main gun originally mounted in the T-35 Model 1932 series was designated the PS-3 76.2mm tank gun Model 1927/32 and was a modified version of the towed 76.2mm Model 1927 Infantry Support Gun.

In lieu of a coaxial 7.62mm machine gun, the 76.2mm turret on the T-35 series had a 7.62mm machine gun mounted in the right-hand side forward portion of the turret in a ball mount. The last few production units of the vehicle also had a 7.62mm machine gun fitted in a ball mount in the vehicle's rear turret bustle.

The T-35 series featured four smaller sub-turrets (with limited traverse) arrayed around the four corners of the vehicle's superstructure. Two of the smaller sub-turrets on the original T-35 series had been armed with 37mm tank guns, with the remaining two turrets armed only with a single 7.62mm machine gun.

With the introduction of the T-35 Model 1935, the 37mm guns were replaced by 45mm versions. The original 45mm guns were later replaced by an improved longer-barrelled 45mm tank gun. The two-man 45mm gun-armed turrets on the T-35 Model 1935 were based on the turret design of the BT-5 Fast Tank,

In this German army picture the thickness of the armour is marked on a captured Red Army T-35 Model 1935 heavy tank that has been up-armoured. The tall central turret on the vehicle was armed with a 76.2mm main gun, while two of the sub-turrets were armed with a 45mm gun and the other two with 7.62mm machine guns. (*Patton Museum*)

without the turret bustle. The remaining two one-man 7.62mm machine-gun-armed turrets on the vehicle were copied from the small one-man turrets seen on the Red Army's pre-war light amphibious tanks.

By 1936 another 76.2mm gun designated the KT-28 Model 1927/32 was installed in the T-35 series. Some thought was given to mounting another 76.2mm gun in the T-35 series, designated the 76.2mm L-10 L/26, since it had superior armour penetrating capabilities and had been mounted in the T-28 medium tank. However, since the T-35 series already had two 45mm gun-armed turrets dedicated to anti-tank purposes, the 76.2mm L-10 L/26 was not fitted.

Out of the sixty-one T-35 series tanks built, the last six constructed between 1938 and 1939 were modernized and referred to as the T-35 Model 1938 Heavy Tank. They can be identified by the replacement of the slab-sided turrets seen on the T-35 Model 1935 with newly-designed turrets featuring sloped sides. Armour thickness on the front of the vehicle's turret was also increased with a maximum thickness of 70mm compared to the 30mm found on earlier production units of the vehicle. Vehicle weight on the T-35 Model 1938 is reported to have reached 121,000lb (55mt).

The Red Army did not deploy the T-35 series during the Russo-Finnish War. It seemed to have been generally reserved for use in pre-war parades in Moscow's Red Square where its size and armament array no doubt impressed the assembled visitors. The Red Army's inventory of T-35s would, however, see combat in the early months of the German invasion of the Soviet Union with most being lost to mechanical failure. A few lasted long enough to see use

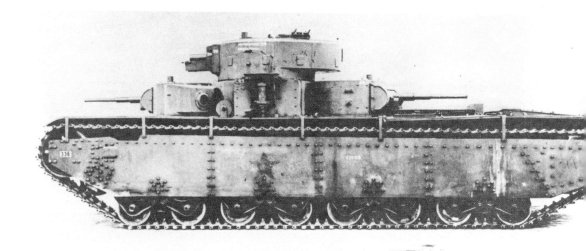

The T-35 Model 1935 shown here was the standard production version of the vehicle. There was an earlier version designated the T-35 Model 1932 that can be identified by the fact that it had only three bogie wheel assemblies on either side of the hull instead of the four seen here. (*Patton Museum*)

Seen here on display at Kubinka is a T-35 Model 1935 tank. The vehicle was 31ft 11in (9.73m) long and 10ft 6in (3.20m) wide with a height of 11ft 3in (3.43m). The operational range of the tank was 93 miles (150km), typical for gasoline-powered tanks of that time. (*Vladimir Yakubov*)

during the defence of Moscow between December 1941 and January 1942.

Development of a suitable replacement for the unsatisfactory T-35 series began in 1938 and involved two different design bureaus. One was headed by Zh. Ya. Kotin and the other by N. Barykov. The original Red Army requirements for this proposed new heavy tank mandated a total of five turrets. This was soon dropped to a three-turret requirement, and with Stalin's last-minute input it went down to two turrets. The larger, uppermost turret with 360 degrees of traverse was to be armed with a 76.2mm gun and a coaxial 7.62mm machine gun, and the smaller bottom turret with more limited traverse was to be armed with a 45mm gun and a coaxial 7.62mm machine gun.

The Kotin-designed contender for the proposed new heavy tank weighed 121,253lb (55mt) and was designated the 'SMK', the abbreviation for Sergey Mironovich Kirov, an early and prominent Bolshevik leader who was assassinated in 1934. The Barykov design bureau's vehicle weighed 129,920lb (65mt) and was called the T-100 or *Sotka*, the Russian slang word for '100'. It, like the Kotin-proposed heavy tank, would mount a 76.2mm gun in its upper turret and a 45mm gun in the lower turret, both being fitted with coaxial 7.62mm machine guns. The maximum armour thickness on the front of the SMK turret was 60mm and 70mm on the front of the T-100 turret.

The two-turret requirement for the new heavy tank troubled the Kotin design

German soldiers are examining what appears to be an abandoned T-35 Model 1935 tank. Not known for their reliability, the majority of T-35 series tanks lost during the early stages of the German invasion of the Soviet Union fell out due to mechanical problems or lack of fuel. (*Patton Museum*)

bureau who felt it was outdated for modern tanks. So they received permission from Stalin to design a heavy tank based on components from their two-turret tank, but featuring only a single turret. The single-turreted heavy tank was to be armed with a 76.2mm main gun. It was referred to as the 'KV Tank' in honour of Marshal of the Soviet Union Klimenti Voroshilov, who was then the People's Commissar for Defence of the Soviet Union and Kotin's father-in-law.

When the three prototype heavy tanks were tested in 1939, it was clear to all that the single-turreted KV was clearly superior to the two-turreted vehicles. To verify the testing results, all three prototypes were sent to participate in the early stages of the Russo-Finnish War. Of the three vehicles that saw combat in Finland, it was the KV that proved to be the most reliable. An added plus was that its maximum armour thickness of 90mm on its turret front made it immune to all the enemy direct-fire weapons it encountered. This demonstration of its combat effectiveness resulted in the decision in December 1939 to approve the vehicle for production as the KV-1.

The original five-man KV-1 weighed 99,207lb (45mt) and used the same diesel-

German soldiers pose next to an abandoned T-35 Model 1935 heavy tank. Obsolete by the time the Second World War began due to its thin armour protection of only 30mm maximum, there was obviously the inherent difficulty in successfully commanding in battle a vehicle with a crew of eleven men. (*Patton Museum*)

powered engine installed in the much lighter T-34. This meant the on-and off-road mobility of the vehicle was inferior to the T-34 it was intended to work alongside; a problem that eventually resulted in the vehicle being restricted to units made up of only KV-1s. The vehicle rode on a torsion bar suspension system. The biggest problem with the KV-1 was the fact that its mechanical reliability proved inferior to that of the T-34.

The first version of the KV-1 series was referred to as the KV-1 Model 1939. It was quickly superseded in production by the improved KV-1 Model 1940 armed with the longer-barrelled F-32 76.2mm main gun. The KV-1 series was also armed with three 7.62mm machine guns. One acted as the coaxial machine gun with another in the front hull. The third machine gun was fitted in a ball mount located in the rear of the vehicle's turret.

An unfounded belief in the spring of 1941 that the German army was upgrading its tank main guns resulted in the KV-1 Model 1940 being fitted with 35mm-thick add-on armour plates bolted to its turret and hull. Later production units of the KV-1 came off the assembly lines with a more thickly-armoured turret that made the addition of add-on armour unnecessary.

The next tank in the KV-1 series was the KV-1 Model 1941. It was this version of the tank that received the F-34 76.2mm gun that had appeared on the T-34

In an effort to keep the T-35 series viable on future battlefields, the Red Army had the last six production units of the vehicle fitted with new turrets that featured sloped armour, as is seen in this picture. In this configuration the vehicle was designated the T-35 Model 1938. (*Patton Museum*)

Model 1941 in February 1941. When mounted on the KV-1 Model 1941, the F-34 76.2mm gun was designated the ZiS-5. The ZiS-5 76.2mm guns were merely an improved version of the F-32 76.2mm gun that had a longer barrel than the previous 76.2mm main gun mounted on the KV-1 series. It can be identified on the KV-1 series because the barrel projected a few inches over the front of the vehicle's hull. Due to temporary shortages, some KV-1 Model 1941s received the F-34 76.2mm gun instead of the ZiS-5 76.2mm version.

Unhappiness with the T-35 heavy tank series led the Red Army to seek out a new heavy tank. One of the three prototype candidates submitted for consideration to the Red Army was the twin-turreted design shown here that was referred to as the T-100. (*Patton Museum*)

Despite their superior level of armour protection, the roughly 500 KV-1 series tanks assigned to the western districts of the Soviet Union in the summer of 1941 did not fare well against the invading German army with the exception of some isolated occasions. The ill-trained crews of the recently-arrived KV-1s were at a serious disadvantage when engaging the better-trained veteran tank crews of the German army. Part of the problem was the poorly-designed crew layout in the KV-1 series turret that had the vehicle commander double as the gun-loader. Adding to the problem was the fact that the KV-1 series vehicle commander did not have an overhead hatch which would have allowed him to monitor the tactical situation around his vehicle when in combat.

Kotin had given some thought to designing and building a brand-new heavy tank referred to as the *Obiekt* 222, which later became known as the KV-3. It would be the replacement for the flawed KV-1 series but retaining the same ZiS-5 76.2mm gun. The KV-3 was initially supposed to be armed with the 107mm ZiS-6 gun, but it was decided that it was too powerful since the Germans didn't have anything that would stand up to the standard 76.2mm tank gun at that point in the war.

Pictured is the single SMK prototype, knocked out in Finland. Field testing conducted in 1940 during the ongoing Russo-Finnish War showed the SMK and another twin-turreted heavy tank prototype known as the T-100 were both ungainly and too complicated to be practical in service. (*Patton Museum*)

Plans had progressed far enough in early 1941 that it was intended for the 156,526-lb (71mt) KV-3 to replace the KV-1 series on the assembly lines beginning in August 1941. The German invasion of the Soviet Union quickly brought an abrupt halt to that plan. As much as some would have liked to have seen the KV-3 fielded, it was recognized that any interruption of the existing production lines would have jeopardized the ability of the Red Army to field enough tanks on the battlefield to make up for the terrible rate of attrition it was experiencing in combat. Only a single prototype of the KV-3 was ever built and it had a maximum armour protection of 100mm on its turret front. The KV-3 prototype hull fitted with a standard KV-1 turret was later committed to combat and eventually destroyed.

Some thought had been given to mounting a new turret on the KV-1 armed with a 107mm main gun. This design concept had been assigned the designation *Obiekt* 220 and would have included adding a new and more powerful engine in the KV-1 hull. Nothing ever came of the project as the Red Army was more interested in the quantity of tanks being built rather than the quality.

There were also plans to develop a couple of super-heavy tanks, designated the KV-4 and KV-5. The KV-4 was to be protected by a maximum armour thickness of 130mm and the KV-5 a maximum armour thickness of 180mm. Both proposed super-heavy tanks were to be armed with a 107mm main gun. The obvious problem with these vehicles would have been their weight, estimated in the case of the KV-5 to be around 370,372-lb (168mt). With the German army overrunning the factory where these impractical projects were being contemplated, work was suspended and never restarted.

The KV-1 Model 1941 was succeeded in service by the KV-1 Model 1942, which featured a more thickly-armoured turret. This armour upgrade came at a price as the powertrain of the KV-1 series had been troublesome since its inception and the additional armour only made the problem worse. In total about 3,800 units of the KV-1 series were built between 1939 and 1943. There was also a flame-thrower variant of the KV-1 series built in small numbers and designated the KV-8. It mounted a 45mm main gun in lieu of the standard 76.2mm main gun to make room for the turret-mounted flame-thrower gun.

Combat experience gained during the Russo-Finnish War had shown that the existing Red Army tanks lacked the firepower necessary to destroy the heavily

Of the three heavy tank designs submitted to the Red Army for consideration in 1939, the only one that made the cut was a single-turreted version of the SMK that would become the KV-1 series. Pictured is a vehicle from the first production batch sometimes referred to as the KV-1 Model 1939 and armed with an L-11 76.2mm main gun in a welded turret. (*Patton Museum*)

A German soldier examines a knocked-out KV-1 Model 1940 armed with a new F-32 76.2mm main gun. It can be identified by the welded armoured collar around the rear portion of the barrel that attached to the cast gun shield and protected the weapon's hydro-pneumatic recuperator. (*Patton Museum*)

reinforced Finnish army bunkers being encountered. At the prodding of a senior general of the Red Army commanding troops in Finland, a new heavy break-through tank was conceived. In the span of two weeks a plan was hatched to mount a newly-designed turret mounting an M-10 152mm howitzer on an unmodified KV-1 series chassis. A prototype of this stop-gap vehicle was ready for testing in January 1940.

The initial prototype and a small number of very early series production units of this new heavy breakthrough tank were referred to as the KV-2 Model 1939. They featured a fairly complex angled turret design. The follow-on production units had a simpler and quicker to build turret design and were designated the KV-2 Model 1940. Production of the KV-2 series, nicknamed the 'Dreadnought' by its crews, began in November 1940 and continued until October 1941 with 334 units completed. Besides its main gun, the KV-2 was armed with three 7.62mm machine guns with the KV-2 Model 1940. Maximum armour thickness on the front of the KV-2 turret was 110mm.

Compared to the typical KV-1 series tank that weighed in at roughly 94,000lb

A KV-1 Model 1940 has been caught in the woods and hit, evident from the smoke coming out of the hull and turret of the vehicle. The tank carried an authorized allotment of 111 76.2mm main gun rounds stored between the turret and hull, with most stored in the hull. (*Patton Museum*)

(43mt), the six-man KV-2 might weigh as much as 114,000lb (52mt). The added 20,000lb (9.1mt) overloaded a chassis that was already plagued by automotive design issues. This made the KV-2's on-and off-road mobility inferior to the KV-1 series. The large, heavy and unbalanced turret on the KV-2 also caused problems in traversing it on anything other than level surfaces.

Some KV-2s were based in the western military districts of the Soviet Union that took the initial invasion blows of the German army. On those occasions where the KV-2 series was encountered by advancing German army units in the summer of 1941, the vehicle's thick armour provided it with immunity to almost every weapon in the German arsenal except the 88mm *FlaK* gun. Fortunately for the German army, the KV-2s were few and far between, with most being lost to mechanical failure or lack of fuel. A small number of KV-2s would survive long enough to see service during the fighting for Stalingrad, which lasted from August 1942 until February 1943.

Following the KV-1 Model 1942 off the production line was another version in the KV-1 series designated the KV-1S. The KV-1S design corrected some of the problems found in the earlier versions of the KV-1 series. Production of the KV-1S began in August 1942 and continued until April 1943 with 1,370 units completed. The suffix 'S' in the designation was the abbreviation for the Russian word *skorostnoi*, which means speedy. As in the entire KV-1 series, there was a coaxial 7.62mm machine gun and a ball mount for a 7.62mm machine gun in the rear of the vehicle's turret.

To improve the on-and off-road performance of the KV-1S, the designers did the only thing possible and thinned out the armour on the vehicle's turret and hull, trading protection for mobility. This brought the vehicle's weight down to 93,695-lb (42.5mt). Maximum armour thickness on the front of the KV-1S turret was 82mm.

There were also powertrain improvements to the KV-1S, especially to the transmission, to improve the vehicle's reliability. Another big improvement on the tank was freeing the vehicle commander from his secondary job as a loader and providing him with an overhead armoured cupola to improve his situational awareness on the battlefield.

German cavalrymen ride past a knocked-out KV-1 Model 1940 tank. Visible on the side of the turret are riveted add-on armour plates that began showing up in April 1940. This took place because of an unfounded belief that more powerful German anti-tank guns were being fielded. (*Patton Museum*)

A German officer poses next to a knocked-out KV-1 Model 1940 tank. The welded armoured turret is fitted with the riveted add-on armour plates. The vehicle was 22ft 2in (6.75m) long, 10ft 11in (3.33m) wide and 8ft 11in (2.72m) tall. (*Patton Museum*)

The KV-1S also featured a smaller, more streamlined turret than its predecessors. However, it still retained the 76.2mm ZiS-5 main gun of the earlier versions of the vehicle. This was not a popular decision with General M.E. Katukov, one of the best and brightest tank commanders of the Red Army. He correctly foretold in a meeting with Stalin in September 1942 that the German army would soon field a next generation of tanks that would be immune to the 76.2mm main guns on the KV-1 series as well as the T-34.

As soon as Katukov's predication was verified in August 1942 by the appearance of the German Tiger E heavy tank, production of the KV-1S began tailing off. Only 452 units were built in 1943 before the entire KV-1 series was cancelled. There had been an attempt to mount the S-31 85mm main gun in the KV-1S, but the arrangement proved impractical as the turret was too small to fit the larger gun.

The need for a replacement for the KV-1 series had not been ignored by the Red Army. By the autumn of 1942 the KV-1 series was clearly seen by all as a failure in service. A number of design projects were in the works to come up with a new tank under the umbrella designation KV-13. It was intended that the

On display at the Armoured Vehicle Museum located in Parola, Finland is the sole surviving example of a KV-1E, captured by the Finnish army during the Second World War. The add-on armour plates were also affixed to the vehicle's upper hull as seen here. (*Andreas Kirchhoff*)

KV-13 could replace both the T-34 and the KV-1 series. However, when the German army began fielding the next generation of up-armoured medium and heavy tanks between January and June 1943, the KV-13 was not far enough along in the developmental cycle to be rushed into production.

It was a team of engineers working under the direction of Kotin who managed to save the day by coming up with a new heavy tank design based on the KV-1 series. A prototype was shown to Stalin in August 1943 and with his approval was ordered into production. The vehicle was originally referred to as the izd.237. The prefix 'izd' is the abbreviation for *izdeliye* in Russian and translated means 'item'. Upon being approved for production, the izd.237 became the IS-85, the prefix 'IS' being the Russian abbreviation for Iosef Stalin.

The IS-85 sported a brand-new three-man turret design that did not burden the vehicle commander with any secondary duties and provided him with an overhead armoured cupola as first seen on the KV-1S. Armament of the IS-85 was the new D-5T 85mm main gun. The IS-85 retained the coaxial 7.62mm machine gun and the rear turret-mounted 7.62mm machine gun as seen on all of the KV-1 series tanks.

Pictured on display at the Central Armed Forces Museum located in Moscow, Russia is this KV-1 Model 1941 armed with a new 76.2mm main gun. Vehicles with this gun can be distinguished by its longer barrel and new design for the cast gun shield. This particular vehicle retains the turret from the Model 1940. (*Vladimir Yakubov*)

The powertrain in the IS-85 was an improved version of that on the KV-1 series, and the suspension system was also very similar. The biggest design departure for the IS-85 from the KV-1 series was the much better-shaped hull that offered superior ballistic protection. The hull design for the IS-85 came from design work done for the KV-13 and dispensed with the bow machine-gunner in the front hull, bringing the crew down to four men.

Because it would take time for the factories and foundries to tool-up for production of the IS-85, Stalin also gave his approval in August 1943 for the production of an interim heavy tank mounting the new IS-85 turret on a widened KV-1S hull. This stop-gap vehicle was designated the KV-85 and 130 units were built between September and November 1943. It was the last version of the KV-1 series to see combat. The turret front armour of the KV-85 was 160mm thick.

To make room for the larger main gun rounds in the !01,411-lb (46mt) KV-85, the bow machine-gunner in the front hull was again dispensed with, leaving a crew of only four men.

Visibility out of the KV-1 series with all the hatches closed for combat was extremely poor and no doubt contributed to the driver of the vehicle pictured winding up in a large ditch. The vehicle was 22ft 8in (6.91m) long, had a width of 10ft 11in (3.33m) and was 9ft 7in (2.92m) tall. (*Patton Museum*)

Curious German soldiers are pictured on top of a still-smouldering KV-1 tank. Besides a 76.2mm main gun, the vehicle was armed with three 7.62mm machine guns, one of which was fitted in a ball mount at the rear of the turret bustle as seen here. (*Patton Museum*)

Production of the IS-85 began at the end of 1943 and continued until early 1944 with 107 units completed. However, doubts about the ability of the 85mm main gun to effectively deal with the armour on the late-war German tanks led to the decision to look at a larger, more potent main gun on the vehicle.

The weapon chosen in November 1943 for a couple of different reasons was a 122mm artillery piece designated the A-19. Firstly, there was then a large supply of these guns and their ammunition available and secondly, the weapon had performed well when engaging German Panther medium tanks and Tiger E heavy tanks at the battle of Kursk in July 1943. It also proved possible to shoe-horn the enormous weapon into the same gun mount used for the 85mm main gun on the IS-85. The modified A-19 122mm gun mounted in the IS-85 became the D-25T and was eventually fitted with a large double-baffle muzzle brake.

Successful testing of the D-25T 122mm gun mounted in the IS-85 turret in November 1943 led to a quick decision to place this combination into production. The vehicle was originally called the IS-122 but this was soon changed to the IS-2 Model 1944, at which point the IS-85 was rechristened the IS-1 Model 1943. Some IS-1s were later rearmed with the D-25T 122mm gun, thus becoming an IS-2.

Like the KV-1 series, the IS-2 had a coaxial 7.62mm machine gun with another 7.62mm machine gun in a ball mount in the rear of the vehicle's turret. There was also a fixed forward-firing 7.62mm machine gun in the front hull operated

Several KV-1 Model 1941 heavy tanks armed with the ZiS-5 76.2mm main gun are pictured in a wood line. They retain the M1940 turret. The KV-1 series tanks were all seriously compromised in service by engine and transmission problems that proved much more serious than those encountered with the T-34 series. (*Bob Fleming*)

Pictured is a knocked-out KV-1 Model 1941 with a new welded up-armoured turret that can be identified by the squared-off shape under the turret overhang. The original welded armoured turrets on the KV-1 series bent around the bottom of the turret overhang from a point mid-way on the lower turret. (*Bob Fleming*)

by the driver with a remote control. A new addition to Red Army tanks of the Second World War was the mounting of a 12.7mm machine gun on the IS-2 vehicle commander's cupola for use against aerial and ground targets.

The initial 150 production units of the four-man IS-2 rolled off the factory floor in February 1944. They were not placed into front-line service with the T-34 series but organized into special élite units. These units were in reserve until there was a large offensive operation against the German army, in which case they would form the armoured spearhead of the initial assault wave. Maximum armour thickness on the front of the IS-2 turret was 160mm.

Despite its large size, the armour penetration potency of the 122mm main gun on the IS-2 was not much more than that of the 75mm main gun on the Panther medium tank. Obviously, when firing at a non-armoured target, the high-explosive round of the IS-2 was much more effective due to its size. The IS-2 was a fairly effective weapon on the Eastern Front during its time in service.

The biggest fault with the mounting of the 122mm main gun in the 101,411-lb (46mt) IS-2 was the size of its ammunition. As a complete round would have been too heavy for a single loader, it was made separate, with the projectile

To speed up production, Soviet industry introduced a cast armour turret in 1942 as is seen here on a KV-1 Model 1941. Armour thickness on this new cast armour turret was equal to that of the welded armour turret version of the Model 1941. The turret frontal armour was 100mm thick and the turret sides 75mm thick. (*Bob Fleming*)

going into the weapon's breech first, followed by the cartridge case containing the propellant. Combined with the cramped interior of the IS-2, this meant the vehicle could only carry twenty-eight main gun rounds. By way of comparison, the KV-1S carried 114 rounds of main gun ammunition and the IS-1 had a main gun ammunition load of fifty-nine rounds.

In spite of some design shortcomings, the IS-2 proved extremely popular with Red Army tankers and more were requested. This led to an improved version with a newly-designed front hull glacis that offered a superior level of ballistic protection due its sloped design in comparison to the stepped glacis on earlier IS-2s. Another improvement was the replacement of the main gun's manually-operated screw-type breech with a semi-automatic breech block, which increased the gun's rate of fire from roughly one round per minute up to two rounds per minute. There was also a new wider gun shield fitted. These improved vehicles were referred to as the IS-2 Model 1944. By the time production ended in 1945 a total of 3,854 units of the IS-2 series had been built.

Even while production of the IS-2 series continued, the Red Army sought out the next-generation heavy tank. The design benchmark set for the IS-2's replacement was that the vehicle had to be able to resist fire on its front hull and turret from the armour-piercing projectiles fired by the 88mm KwK43 gun mounted on the German Tiger B heavy tank. The standard armour-piercing projectile fired from the KwK43 gun had a muzzle velocity of 3,280ft per second and could penetrate 132mm of armour sloped at 30 degrees at a range of 2,187yds.

To optimize the ability of the replacement for the IS-2 to resist penetration by high-velocity armour-piercing projectiles, the Russian designers had come up with a large, thickly-armoured and highly-sloped hemispherical turret. It was a far cry from the more slab-sided turret on the IS-2. Maximum armour thickness on the front of the turret of this new heavy tank was 230mm. The two thick, sharply-angled armour plates welded together at the front hull of the vehicle that formed the glacis had a maximum armour thickness of 120mm.

The driver of the KV-1 series tanks sat in the centre of the front hull slightly to the right with the radio operator/bow machine-gunner to his left. Pictured is a KV-1 Model 1941 with a cast armour turret that is on display at the Armoured Vehicle Museum located in Parola, Finland. (*Andreas Kirchhoff*)

The prototype of the IS-2's replacement was shown to a senior commander of the Red Army's armoured forces in December 1944 and met with his excited approval. With input coming from two different design bureaus it would be designated the *Kirovets-1*, with ten pilot vehicles ordered for testing by the following month. Eventually the vehicle would be designated the IS-3. The first examples rolled off the factory floor in late May 1945, too late to see combat in the Second World War. Production of the IS-3 would continue until the middle of 1946 with 2,311 vehicles eventually completed.

Despite the new hull and turret design, the powertrain for the IS-3 was only a slightly improved version of that in the IS-2. It would also retain the four-man crew layout of its predecessor, and the D-25T 122mm main gun with its separate loading main gun ammunition. Due to the highly-sloped turret design of the IS-3, there was no turret bustle where main gun projectiles could be stored as on the IS-2. The twenty-eight main gun projectiles were therefore stored along the inside of the turret walls.

Like the IS-2, the IS-3 had a coaxial 7.62mm machine gun. Not seen on the IS-3

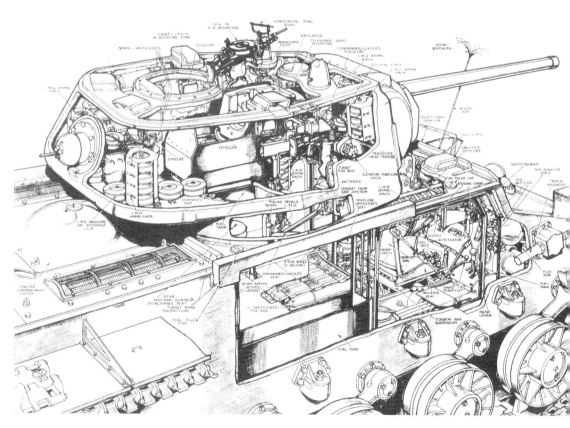

From a Second World War British army document appears this line illustration listing the various parts and components of a KV-1 Model 1941 tank with a cast armoured turret. (*Patton Museum*)

was the relatively useless 7.62mm machine gun fitted in a ball mount at the rear of the vehicle turret, as was standard on the KV-1 and IS-2 series. As with the IS-2 series, there was a 12.7mm machine gun on the IS-3 vehicle commander's cupola for use against aerial and ground targets.

The 110,972-lb (50mt) IS-3 was debuted at a victory parade held in Berlin, Germany on 7 September 1945, when fifty-two of them roared past the assembled visitors, much to the astonishment of the Western Allies who didn't know the monsters existed. Such was the shock at seeing a vehicle with modern design features that it would influence decades of tank development by the NATO armies to counter its potential on some future battlefield. In reality, the IS-3 was far from the perfect tank. Due to the haste with which the vehicle had been rushed into production, it was besieged by a host of design problems, mostly automotive, that were never resolved, even in the post-war era.

Later production KV-1 Model 1941 tanks with welded up-armoured turrets can be identified from the rear by the angled, instead of rounded, rear hull upper decks. This feature is clearly evident on this knocked-out KV-1 Model 1941 tank with a welded turret that has been turned into overhead cover for a German soldier's bunker. (*Patton Museum*)

Like the T-34 series, the KV-1 series tanks had their transmissions located behind their diesel engines as is evident in this overhead picture of a KV-1 Model 1941 with a cast turret. Notice the rounded rear hull upper deck that marked the early production units of the KV-1 Model 1941. (*Patton Museum*)

A factory overhauling KV-1 Model 1941 tanks with both cast and welded armoured turrets. Improved German anti-tank weapons forced the thickening of the armour on later production cast turret KV-1 Model 1941 tanks. These can be identified by the fairing at the bottom of the turret side walls and the angled rear hull upper deck. (*Bob Fleming*)

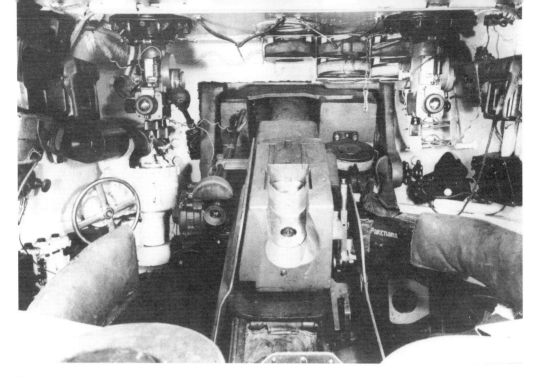

This picture shows the interior of a cast armoured turret from a KV-1 Model 1941 tank. The vehicle's gunner position was on the left-hand side of the main gun and the vehicle's commander/loader position on the right-hand side. (*Patton Museum*)

In this image of the rear turret bustle of a KV-1 Model 1941 tank can be seen the 7.62mm machine gun and the various drum magazine holders for the weapon. On either side of the rear turret interior can be seen storage racks for 76.2mm main gun rounds. (*Patton Museum*)

This picture was taken inside a KV-1 Model 1941 tank from under the breech ring of the vehicle's 76.2mm main gun looking forward into the front hull. Visible is the driver's periscope as well as his instrument panel. The dark-coloured metal conduit in the centre of the picture carries electrical cables to the turret. (*Patton Museum*)

A comparison photograph of a KV-1 Model 1941 with a cast armoured turret and a United States army M4A4 medium tank with a cast armoured turret. The M4A4 was 9ft (2.74m) tall. (*Patton Museum*)

A German army intelligence photograph of a captured flame-thrower version of the KV-1 Model 1940 tank referred to as the KV-8. To make room for the flame-thrower, the original 76.2mm main gun was replaced by a much smaller 45mm gun to provide the vehicle crew with a limited ability to defend themselves against tanks. (*Patton Museum*)

To destroy heavily-fortified bunkers, the Red Army decided it needed a heavy tank armed with a 152mm howitzer. The vehicle was designated the KV-2 and an early production unit is seen here. The first few production vehicles had the turret sides angled inward to the front of the turret as seen here. (*Patton Museum*)

On display at the Central Armed Forces Museum located in Moscow, Russia is this standard production version of the KV-2 with a much simplified slab-sided turret and new-style gun shield. The six-man vehicle was 12ft 11in (3.93m) tall. (*Vladimir Yakubov*)

Pictured is an abandoned KV-2 with its turret pointed over its rear hull. Due to the size of the main gun rounds it could only store thirty-six of them within the tank's hull and turret, with the majority being stored on racks in the turret. (*Patton Museum*)

For removal or replacement of the 152mm howitzer and the loading of the massive main gun rounds in the KV-2 there was a large armoured door in the rear of the vehicle's enormous turret as seen here. Also fitted to the rear of the KV-2 turret was a ball mount for a 7.62mm machine gun. (*Patton Museum*)

A German soldier poses with a high-explosive projectile from a knocked-out or abandoned KV-2. The tank's 152mm howitzer high-explosive projectile travelled at 1,430ft per second, which in theory would penetrate 72mm of armour. There was also a special concrete-piercing projectile for pillbox destruction. (*Patton Museum*)

An object of curiosity to the German soldiers pictured is this knocked-out KV-2 that has taken numerous hits to its large turret. One of the hits penetrated the 152mm howitzer barrel. (*Patton Museum*)

Seen here on display at the Central Armed Forces Museum located in Moscow, Russia is a KV-1S. The vehicle was a much-improved and lighter version of the standard KV-1 series tank with a newly-designed turret but still retaining a 76.2mm main gun. The hull of this vehicle is a reconstruction. (*Vladimir Yakubov*)

To rectify the problem of the KV-1S tank being under-gunned, there was an attempt to mount an 85mm main gun in the turret. This arrangement did not prove practical as the turret of the KV-1S proved too small. That experimental prototype survived and is seen here at Kubinka. (*Vladimir Yakubov*)

With the failure of up-gunning the KV-1S tank with an 85mm main gun, it was decided as a stop-gap measure to take a KV-1S hull and mount on it a turret originally intended for the IS-1 heavy tank. The new turret mounted an 85mm gun and the vehicle seen here was designated as the KV-85. (*Patton Museum*)

One of the key improvements of the KV-85 seen here was the rearrangement of the turret crew positions. The vehicle commander was absolved of the loader's role and the rear hull machine-gunner was given that job. The vehicle was 28ft 2in (8.58m) long and 10ft 8in (3.25m) wide with a height of 9ft 6in (2.90m). (*Bob Fleming*)

The replacement for the KV-1S and the KV-85 heavy tanks was the IS-2 heavy tank armed with a 122mm main gun. A captured example is pictured here and marked by the Germans with the thickness of the armour. The IS-2 featured both a redesigned hull and turret with a host of powertrain improvements. (*Tank Museum*)

A German soldier is looking over a knocked-out early production IS-2 that has no doubt suffered from its on-board ammunition being detonated as the gun shield has been blown out of position. The vehicle features a very large double-baffle muzzle brake to retard recoil. (*Patton Museum*)

An early production IS-2 tank is seen here on display at the National War and Resistance Museum of the Netherlands at Overloon. An identifying feature of early production vehicles is the stepped glacis that it inherited from the experimental KV-13 'universal tank' and narrow gun shield. (*Frank Schulz*)

The transmission access hatches are visible in this picture of the IS-2 on display at Overloon. The armour side plates were 90mm thick. The rear hull armour was 60mm thick. Visible is the ball mount for a 7.62mm machine gun in the rear turret bustle. The vehicle was 32ft 6in (9.90m) long, 10ft 2in (3.09m) wide and 8ft 11in (2.72m) tall. *(Frank Schulz)*

The vehicle commander's cupola on an IS-2 is shown here. The crew of the vehicle consisted of only four men: vehicle commander, gunner, loader and driver. The radio operator/bow machine-gunner's position was dispensed with. Instead there was a fixed, forward-firing 7.62mm machine gun in the right front hull. (*Frank Schultz*)

A Red Army officer briefs the crews of his late production IS-2 tanks at the end of the war in Europe. Due to the weight of the projectile and propellant, it was decided to make the 122mm main gun rounds for the IS-2 separate-loading, which restricted the rate of fire to only two or three rounds per minute. (*Patton Museum*)

Later production IS-2 tanks can be identified by the sloping front glacis and the wider gun shield and are sometimes referred to as the IS-2 Model 1944. This particular vehicle is on display at Kubinka. Due to the size of the 122mm main gun rounds there was only storage space inside the vehicle for twenty-eight of them. (*Vladimir Yakubov*)

On display somewhere in the former Soviet Union is this late production IS-2M tank modernized post-war as indicated by the storage compartments built into the right side of the upper hull sides. These do not appear on wartime vehicles. (*Patton Museum*)

On display at Kubinka is this modernized IS-2M tank. Post-war, the vehicles were rebuilt to store thirty-five main gun rounds and had a number of other improvements made. The Soviet Union would supply the IS-2M to Red China, Cuba and North Korea during the Cold War. (*Vladimir Yakubov*)

The replacement for the IS-2 tank was the IS-3 heavy tank developed during the Second World War. It is shown here in Berlin during a September 1945 victory parade. Its sleek, low-slung appearance and huge 122mm main gun shocked the Western Allies who had nothing that could confront it on equal terms. (*Patton Museum*)

At Kubinka during an open-house event is this IS-3 tank modernized during the post-war era into the IS-3M. The IS-3 did not see combat during the Second World War with the Red Army. However, during the Hungarian uprising in 1956 the Soviet Army employed a small number of IS-3Ms against the anti-communist revolutionaries. (*R. Bazalevsky*)

A number of Egyptian army IS-3M tanks were captured by the Israeli army during the 1967 Six-Day War. The IS-3 and IS-3M were 35ft 3in (10.74m) long and 11ft 3in (3.43m) wide with a vehicle height of 9ft 6in (2.90m). (*Israeli Embassy*)

Belonging to the collection of the United States Army Ordnance Museum is this IS-3M tank. The contraption on top of the vehicle's turret was the frame to mount a 12.7mm machine gun – not seen here – that could be employed against both aerial and ground targets. (*Michael Green*)

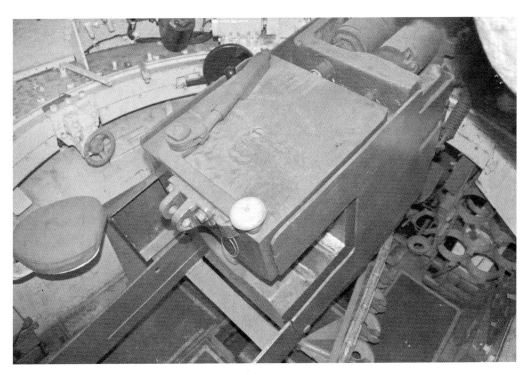

Looking down into the turret of an IS-3M tank can be seen the massive breech ring of the vehicle's 122mm main gun. On the left-hand side of the image is the vehicle commander's seat. The small handle to the left of this is the turret lock. (*Chris Hughes*)

The gunner's position on an IS-3M is seen in this picture. The black handle to the left is the gunner's manual traverse for the main gun. The smaller dark-green handle at the bottom centre of the image is the gunner's manual elevation control for the main gun. (*Chris Hughes*)

Taken from the top of an IS-3M turret looking towards the rear you can see the storage racks for the 122mm projectiles. The propellant was kept in the lower hull. In the centre of the picture is an electrically-operated ventilating blower. (*Chris Hughes*)

This photograph shows the driver's position on an IS-3M tank with his overhead hatch in the open position. Visible is the driver's very simple instrument panel as well as his steering levers on either side of his seat. To his right is the gear-shift lever. (*Chris Hughes*)

Chapter Four

Self-Propelled Guns

The Red Army decided in the early 1930s that it needed self-propelled guns and its artillery branch subsequently came up with a number of prototype models of varying sizes and armament. The only one to be placed in limited production was a variant of the BT-7 series, designated the BT-7A. It was fitted with a 76.2mm regimental howitzer in an oversize turret with 360 degrees of traverse. The suffix 'A' stands for artillery, which in the Russian language is *artilleriya*. A total of 154 units of the BT-7A were built between 1936 and 1938; however, only 134 were fielded, with just eleven of those being fitted with radios. All would be lost in the battles that took place in the summer of 1941.

On display at Kubinka is the single prototype example of the SU-14-2 heavy self-propelled gun, based on the heavily-modified chassis of the T-35 heavy tank. It was armed with a 152mm naval gun and represented pre-war Red Army thought on what a self-propelled gun should look like. (*Vladimir Yakubov*)

On display at the Museum of Artillery, Engineers and Signal Corps located in Saint Petersburg, Russia is this late production SU-76M light self-propelled gun. The vehicle involved the mounting of a 76.2mm field gun on the chassis of a lengthened and modified T-70 light tank. (*Bob Fleming*)

Following the terrible losses in tanks suffered by the Red Army in 1941, what resources it could amass were dedicated to replacing them as quickly as possible. There was little industrial capacity remaining at the time to design and build specialized vehicles such as self-propelled guns. Nevertheless, by the spring of 1942 the Red Army recognized a pressing need for self-propelled guns, also known as mechanized guns, to deal with enemy defensive positions as part of their new mechanized formations.

Strangely enough, it would be the armour branch of the Red Army and not the artillery that initiated the development of self-propelled guns, the first of which would become known as the SU-76 light self-propelled gun. In the Russian language, the words for self-propelled or mechanized are *Samokhodnaya Ustanovka*, with the abbreviation being the prefix 'SU'.

The turretless SU-76 was based on the lengthened chassis of the T-70 light tank and armed with the ZiS-3 76.2mm divisional field gun mounted in the rear

A German soldier crouches next to a knocked-out SU-76M. From the beginning, the vehicle was intended to be an infantry support weapon. However, as the war went on, the increasing armour protection applied to German tanks and self-propelled guns would render it obsolete in its secondary role as a tank destroyer. (*Patton Museum*)

of the vehicle's hull. The weapon was serviced by a crew of three men with the driver located in the front hull. As early units of the T-70 were plagued by powertrain issues, so were the early production units of the SU-76. In both cases the powertrain on the vehicles was redesigned, resulting in improved versions of the vehicles that were identified by the letter 'M' added to their designations. Hence the SU-76 became the SU-76M in the spring of 1943.

Production of the approximately 22,692-lb (11.2mt) SU-76 series began in December 1942 with twenty-six units completed. Almost 2,000 were built in 1943 and over 7,000 in 1944. By the time production of the SU-76 series concluded in 1945, a total of 12,671 units had rolled off the assembly lines of various factories. It would prove to be the second most-produced armoured fighting vehicle in the Red Army's arsenal during the Second World War, next to the T-34 series. As the slightly lighter 22,487-lb (10.2mt) SU-76M entered into front-line service, the earlier SU-76 was withdrawn.

Lacking the armoured protection of the T-34 series, the open-topped SU-76 series was vulnerable to almost every enemy weapon it encountered on the battlefield. The maximum armour thickness on the vehicle's front hull was 35mm. Making matters even worse was the fact that by the time it entered the field in large numbers its main armament was lacking the penetrative abilities to function as a successful anti-tank weapon. This meant the SU-76 series was generally reserved for infantry support duties. Due to its numerous design short-comings the vehicle's crews gave it the unofficial nickname *Suka*, which is the Russian word for 'bitch'.

The chassis of the SU-76 was also modified to serve as a self-propelled anti-aircraft gun, designated the ZSU-37. The prefix 'ZSU' was the abbreviation for the Russian words *Zenitnaya Samokhodnaya Ustanovka*, that translates into self-propelled anti-aircraft gun. The ZSU-37 mounted a 37mm anti-aircraft gun in an open-topped, 360-degree-traversable armoured turret at the rear of the SU-76 chassis. Before production of the ZSU-37 was authorized in 1944 it was decided to use the more reliable SU-76M chassis to mount the weapon. Hampered by a

A column of SU-76M light self-propelled guns is being directed by their unit commander who is standing on top of a T-70 light tank. The SU-76M was 16ft 5in (5.00m) long and 9ft (2.74m) wide with a height of 7ft 3in (2.20m). (*Bob Fleming*)

This picture, taken from the rear of a SU-76M light self-propelled gun, shows the interior of the vehicle. Visible is the 76.2mm gun breech ring and recoil slide. To the left of the breech ring can be seen some of the main gun ammunition storage spaces. (*Bob Fleming*)

slow turret traverse speed which made it difficult to engage fast-moving aircraft, only a few hundred units of the ZSU-37 were built before the end of the Second World War.

The SU-76 series, like the other turretless self-propelled guns to follow it into Red Army service, were manned by tankers and not artillerymen, which was the opposite of the German army arrangement. The vehicles were typically employed as direct-fire assault guns taking on enemy defensive fortifications and also tanks, rather than as indirect fire artillery pieces. They were, in effect, surrogate tanks that were cheaper and easier to build than more complex turreted vehicles.

Turretless self-propelled guns had the ability to carry much larger weapons than would be possible on the existing chassis of the vehicles chosen. This was the same train of thought that the German army implemented with the production of a series of turretless assault guns based on the chassis of the Panzer III medium tank armed with a 75mm gun and known as the *Sturmgeschutz* III (StuG III). Combat encounters with the StuG III had greatly impressed the Red Army and helped push them into fielding similar vehicles.

Built in small numbers during the Second World War for the Red Army was a self-propelled anti-aircraft gun designated the ZSU-37, an example of which is seen here on display at Kubinka. It was armed with a 37mm automatic cannon in a 360-degree traversable turret. (*Vladimir Yakubov*)

Such was the demand for self-propelled guns in early 1943 that the Red Army gave approval to take hundreds of captured German army Panzer III medium tanks and StuG IIIs and convert them into a new Red Army self-propelled gun. This strange combination of German- and Russian-built components was designated the SU-76i Light Self-Propelled Gun. The suffix 'i' was the Russian abbreviation for *inostrannaya*, which is the Russian word for 'foreign'.

The SU-76i consisted of a 76.2mm gun designated the S1, which was basically an F-34 tank gun with some modifications, mounted in the front of an armoured casemate with limited traverse. Unlike the SU-76 series, the SU-76i had overhead armour protection. At least 200 units of the SU-76i were built in 1943. They would see service throughout the year before being withdrawn from front-line service due to a lack of spare parts. In addition to the Su-76i there was also the SG-122 which was a 122mm self-propelled gun based on the chassis of the Panzer III, of which twenty were built.

On display at Kubinka is this SU-122 medium self-propelled gun. It was based on the chassis of the T-34 series tank and mounted a 122mm howitzer in an armoured casemate with limited traverse. The vehicle was 22ft 8in (6.9m) long, 10ft 8in (3.25m) wide and 8ft (2.43m) tall. (*Vladimir Yakubov*)

Following on the heels of the light SU-76 series, the Red Army gave approval in the summer of 1942 to develop a medium self-propelled gun. It would be based on the chassis of the T-34 and be armed with the M-30 122mm howitzer mounted in the front of an armoured casemate with limited traverse. The vehicle was designated as the SU-122 Medium Self-Propelled Howitzer, with production beginning in December 1942.

The SU-122 had a five-man crew who were protected by a maximum of 45mm of armour on its front hull. A lack of success on the battlefield due to the poor penetrative ability of its tank-killing round led to production of the SU-122 being cancelled in mid-1943 in favour of other more effective self-propelled guns then entering service. In total, 1,148 units of the 66,122-lb (30.9mt) SU-122 were completed.

In response to the Tiger E heavy tank threat, a quick-fix solution was conceived that involved taking the chassis of the KV-1 heavy tank and mounting the 152mm ML-20 gun/howitzer in the front of an armoured casemate with limited traverse. The new 100,309-lb (45.5mt) self-propelled gun was designated

A Red Army SU-122 medium self-propelled gun is shown knocked-out in combat in this dramatically-composed photograph. It fired either a HEAT round that in theory could penetrate 200mm of armour, or a standard HE round out to a range of 12,904 yards. (*Patton Museum*)

the SU-152 and had a five-man crew. The maximum armour thickness on the vehicle's front hull was 60mm. The 152mm ML-20 gun/howitzer was fitted with a large, very distinctive multi-slot muzzle brake.

Production of the SU-152 began in February 1943 with the first units formed entering front-line service in May of that same year. It was the sheer bulk of the anti-tank rounds fired from its main armament that allowed it to penetrate the thick, vertical armour plates of the German Tiger E heavy tank, or the well-sloped frontal armour on the early versions of the German Panther medium tank.

Due to the ability of the SU-152 to successfully take on and destroy late-war German armoured fighting vehicles, it was nicknamed the *Zvierboy*, which translates as 'animal hunter'. The Red Army would stop production of the SU-152 by the end of 1943 with 704 units having been constructed.

As production of the less-than-successful KV-1 heavy tank was ordered halted in April 1943, the Red Army began looking at using the chassis of the new IS-2 heavy tank as a platform to build a replacement vehicle for the SU-152. Rather

A German army picture of a captured SU-122 medium self-propelled gun marked with both the thickness of the vehicle's armour at various locations and the slope of the plates. (*Patton Museum*)

than limit their replacement heavy self-propelled gun to just the 152mm ML-20 gun/howitzer as fitted in the SU-152, the new self-propelled gun mount was also designed to be fitted with a 122mm gun, designated the A-19, as there was a plentiful supply of these guns and their ammunition. Depending on the weapon fitted, the new self-propelled guns were designated the ISU-152 or the ISU-122. Unlike the ISU-152, the gun on the ISU-122 did not have a muzzle brake.

At some point during the production of the ISU-122, a decision was made to improve the vehicle's rate of fire. This was accomplished by replacing the original manually-operated breechblock with a semi-automatic breechblock that had been originally designed for the IS-2 heavy tank. The improved A-19 122mm gun was assigned the designation D-25S. Vehicles mounting the new gun were designated the ISU-122S, and also featured a new smaller gun shield as well as a large double-baffle muzzle brake.

The weapons on the 101,412-lb (46mt) ISU-152 and the 100,309-lb (45.5mt) ISU-122 were mounted in the front of an armoured casemate that provided them with limited traverse. The ISU-152 and the ISU-122/ISU-122S had a taller casemate whose sides were sloped at less of an angle than their predecessor, the SU-152. The maximum armour thickness on the front hull of the near-identical ISU-152 and ISU-122 was 90mm.

Belonging to the collection at Kubinka is this SU-152 heavy self-propelled gun armed with a 152mm gun/howitzer. The vehicle was rushed into service as a counter to the German army Tiger E heavy tank that had first appeared on the Eastern Front in autumn 1942. (*Vladimir Yakubov*)

Production of the ISU-152 and ISU-122 began in late 1943. By the time production ceased in 1945, a total of 1,665 units of the ISU-152 had been completed and 1,735 units of the ISU-122. There were also 675 units of the ISU-122S constructed by the end of the Second World War. On the battlefield, all three of these vehicles shared the same tactical role in tackling German defensive fortifications and providing over-watch protection for T-34 series medium tanks. The ISU-122 and ISU-122S were preferred for engaging enemy tanks at longer ranges, and the ISU-152 for dealing with enemy fortifications due to its much larger high-explosive round.

To supplement the ISU-152 and ISU-122 dual-purpose main guns, the Red Army also fielded tank destroyers dedicated strictly to the anti-tank role. The initial version was designated the SU-85 and entered production in August 1943 as an antidote to the German fielding of the Tiger E heavy tank and early versions of the Panther medium tank series. The SU-85 was primarily based on the now-redundant chassis of the SU-122 and mounted the new D-5T 85mm main gun in a fixed forward-firing position in an armoured casemate with limited traverse.

In its role as a dedicated tank destroyer, the 65,256-lb (30mt) SU-85 assumed

Rohr der alten Feldhaubitze 15,2

Fahrgestell des alten KW i

Notice the very large, multi-slot muzzle brake in this German army photograph of a captured SU-152 heavy self-propelled gun. The chassis used for the vehicle was the KV-1S. The vehicle's main gun fired an anti-tank round that could, in theory, penetrate 110mm of armour at 2,187 yards. (*Patton Museum*)

the over-watch position to protect the less well-armed T34/76 medium tanks. Lacking any machine guns, the SU-85 was not suitable for close-in fighting. Production of the four-man SU-85 was discontinued in the summer of 1944 as the T-34-85 medium tank was now entering front-line service in large numbers and the SU-85 was no longer needed. A total of 2,050 units of the SU-85 were completed. Maximum armour thickness on the vehicle was 45mm.

The Red Army replacement for the SU-85 was the four-man SU-100. It was based on the same T-34 series chassis as the SU-85, with a modified gun shield that allowed the fitting of the 100mm D-10S gun that was more than capable of penetrating the frontal armour on late-war German medium and heavy tanks.

The 69,665-lb (32mt) SU-100 was typically assigned to élite specialized units formed in December 1944 and held under tank army control to provide a defence against the appearance of German tank units equipped with the Tiger B heavy tank. The vehicle was first deployed in large numbers in January 1945 during the fighting in Poland. Like the SU-85, the maximum armour thickness on the vehicle's front hull was 45mm.

To make room for the larger breech ring of the 100mm gun in the SU-100, the vehicle's commander's station on the right side of the vehicle was extended outward from the side of the armoured casemate. This extension on the SU-100 was topped off with a vehicle commander's cupola similar to that found on the T-34-85 medium tank. Due to production problems in the manufacture of 100mm D-10S guns, some of the early SU-100s were armed with 85mm guns and designated the SU-85M.

Production of the SU-100 began in September 1944 and continued until 1945 with 2,355 units built. Production of the vehicle continued after the war in the Soviet Union until 1947. A slightly modified version of the SU-100 was licence-built in Czechoslovakia in the 1950s.

Like ancient beasts ascending from the primordial bog, a couple of SU-152 heavy self-propelled guns are pictured exiting a river. The vehicle was 29ft 4in (8.94m) long and 10ft 8in (3.25m) wide with a height of 8ft (2.44m). (*Bob Fleming*)

A German army NCO cradles a projectile from the destroyed SU-152 heavy self-propelled gun in the background of the picture. Due to the weight and size of the rounds fired by the vehicle's 152mm gun/howitzer, they were separate-loading rounds, which meant the rate of fire was only two rounds per minute. (*Patton Museum*)

German soldiers look over a destroyed SU-152 heavy self-propelled gun that probably suffered a catastrophic internal explosion when the on-board ammunition was detonated by a penetrating enemy projectile. Because of the size of the 152mm main gun rounds, the vehicle could only carry twenty of them. (*Patton Museum*)

Pictured is the inside of a Soviet factory building the SU-152 heavy self-propelled gun. The first unit of vehicles was formed in May 1943 and would take part in the fighting during the Battle of Kursk in July 1943. Due to their success in destroying Panther and Tiger tanks, they received the nickname *Zvierboy* ('animal hunter'). (*Bob Fleming*)

The replacement for the SU-152 heavy self-propelled gun was the ISU-152 heavy self-propelled gun seen here at Kubinka. It was based on the chassis of the IS-2 heavy tank with an armoured casemate that was higher than that on the SU-152 with less steeply-sloped sides. (*Vladimir Yakubov*)

Six ISU-152 heavy self-propelled guns are pictured during a pause in the fighting as attested by the heavily-damaged building they are parked in front of. The vehicle was 29ft 7in (9.01m) long, had a width of 10ft (3.04m) and a height of 8ft 1in (2.46m). (*Bob Fleming*)

This is a close-up view of the rear engine deck of an ISU-152 heavy self-propelled gun. The vehicle was powered by the same liquid-cooled 12-cylinder diesel engine that powered the IS-2 heavy tank and gave it a maximum operational range of 150 miles (241km). (*Bob Fleming*)

Belonging to the collection of vehicles on display at the Imperial War Museum located near Duxford, England is this ISU-152 heavy self-propelled gun in the markings of the Polish army. The vehicle remained in production until 1955. Modernized post-war versions of it were designated the ISU-152K. (*Christophe Vallier*)

The crewmen of an ISU-152 heavy self-propelled gun are shown asking somebody for directions to the front line. The typical role of the ISU-152 during the Second World War was to support offensive breakthroughs and to neutralize enemy strongpoints and anti-tank defences with its large-calibre HE rounds. (*Bob Fleming*)

In 1943 there was a shortage of 152mm guns/howitzers to arm the ISU-152 heavy self-propelled gun. What there was a surplus of at that time were 122mm guns and ammunition. A decision was therefore made to mount the 122mm gun in the ISU-152 hull, which created the ISU-122 seen here on parade. (*Bob Fleming*)

The crew of an ISU-122 and some infantrymen pose for the photographer. The vehicle's primary role was long-range fire support for the T-34 series medium tanks against German heavy tanks and defensive works. (*Bob Fleming*)

The Red Army never stopped looking ahead to the next generation of self-propelled guns. As the IS-3 heavy tank was entering service, it was decided to come up with a self-propelled gun version of the vehicle seen here, designated the Object 704. It never entered into production. (*Vladimir Yakubov*)

The introduction of the German Tiger tank not only pushed along the development and fielding of the SU-152 heavy self-propelled gun, it also sparked the development and fielding in August 1943 of the SU-85 tank destroyer. A destroyed example of the SU-85 is seen here being inspected by German soldiers. (*Bob Fleming*)

German soldiers are seen on top of a captured Red Army SU-85 tank destroyer that they must be considering using in combat due to the numerous German markings on the vehicle. The SU-85's primary battlefield role was the over-watch protection of first-generation T-34 series tanks armed with 76.2mm main guns. (*Bob Fleming*)

Visible is an SU-85 in German markings and a captured T-34 Model 1943 late production medium tank with a vehicle commander's cupola. Notice the empty frames for holding the external fuel tanks on the left-hand side of the vehicle. The SU-85 is not much lower in height than the T-34 tank parked behind. It was 26ft 9in (8.15m) long and 9ft 10in (3.00m) wide with its height at 8ft (2.44m). (*Patton Museum*)

As soon as the T-34-85 was introduced into service it made no sense to continue production of the SU-85. Fortunately it proved possible to mount a 100mm main gun into the SU-85 hull. This new combination was designated the SU-100. The vehicle seen here is a post-war-built Czech version. (*Michael Green*)

This photograph shows the cast armour gun shield on this post-war-built Czech version of the SU-100 at the Tank Museum, Bovington. It differs in shape from that seen on the SU-85 tank destroyer. This feature and the increased length of the gun are useful in telling the two vehicles apart. (*Patton Museum*)

Another identifying feature of the SU-100 was the addition of a new commander's cupola. Modernized wartime vehicles or post-war-built SU-100s are often seen with a large metal stowage box on the right-hand side of the front hull. Both these features appear on the SU-100 pictured. (*Department of Defense*)

An important external detail seen on both wartime and post-war-built SU-100s is the extension under the vehicle commander's cupola that projects out from the right front side of the vehicle as seen here. It was intended to provide the vehicle commander with more room as the breech of the 100mm main gun took up more space in the vehicle's fighting compartment. (*Chris Hughes*)

Chapter Five

Miscellaneous Armoured Fighting Vehicles

The Russian Imperial Army would use a wide variety of armoured cars during the First World War, including a number of British versions. Unhappiness with these British-designed vehicles eventually caused the Imperial Army to turn towards using home-grown armoured cars built on the chassis of foreign-designed and built vehicles, including British, French, Italian and even American products. This reliance on foreign manufacturers for the chassis

The Russian Imperial Army acquired a number of foreign-designed and built armoured cars during the First World War. One of these was the British Armstrong-Whitworth seen here. Some of these non-indigenous-designed and built armoured cars would eventually find their way into Red Army service after being captured from the Whites. (*Patton Museum*)

A very popular British armoured car copied by the Russian Imperial Army during the First World War was a twin-turreted vehicle designed and built by the Austin Motor Company. The copy was known as the 'Putilov-Austin' and an example is seen here at Kubinka. It also saw service with the Red Army. (*Vladimir Yakubov*)

of their gasoline-engine-powered armoured cars seriously limited the numbers that could be built and maintained. Eventually, the Red Army would inherit all these vehicles as well as those left behind by Allied forces that had been in Russia to assist the Imperial Army.

The first post-Civil War armoured car built in large numbers for the Red Army was designated the BA-27 heavy armoured car of which 217 were built in 1927. Originally the armoured body armed with a turret-mounted 37mm main gun was based on the first Russian-built truck designated the AMO-F-15. Later production units of the gasoline-powered vehicle were based on the chassis of a Ford Motors truck chassis that was better suited to handle the weight of the vehicle.

It was not until the 1930s that the Red Army sought to field more modern armoured cars in large numbers. The first of these was the two-man FAI light armoured car based on the Ford Motors Model A chassis. It appeared in 1932 and was armed with a turret-mounted 7.62mm machine gun. The vehicle weighed 4,409lb (2mt) and had a maximum armour thickness of 8mm on the front of its turret.

The FAI light armoured car was replaced in 1936 by the very similar-looking BA-20 that was based on the chassis of the GAZ-M1 car which in turn was a copy of a 1933 Ford Motors car. Classified as a light armoured car, the 5,511-lb (2.5mt) BA-20 was armed with a turret-mounted 7.62mm machine gun. There was also a version of the vehicle that could be configured to ride on rails and was designated as the BA-20ZhD. An improved version of the vehicle was referred to as the BA-20M. Maximum armour thickness on the BA-20 series of armoured cars was 10mm on the front of their turrets.

To complement its light armoured cars, the Red Army would take into service a series of gasoline-engine-powered heavy armoured cars in the 1930s. One of these was the BA-1 armed with a turret-mounted 37mm main gun and a single 7.62mm machine gun. The letter 'I' stood for the Izhorsky plant that had produced the vehicle. Because it proved under-armed and overweight, it remained in production for only a short time before being replaced by the BA-3 armed with a modified turret taken from the T-26 Model 1933 light tank armed with a 45mm main gun and a coaxial 7.62mm machine gun. The four-man BA-3 would eventually be replaced on the production line by the very similar BA-6. The BA-3 weighed 14,771-lb (6.7mt) and the BA-6 weighed 12,566-lb (5.7mt).

By the 1930s the Red Army was beginning to field its own locally-designed and built armoured cars. One of these was the BA-20 light armoured car seen here taking part in a pre-Second World War parade. The vehicle in the foreground is radio-equipped as is evident from its metal frame antenna. (*Tank Museum*)

A column of Red Army BA-20 armoured cars is being led by three motorcyclists. The Red Army defined armoured cars as 'light' when armed only with machine guns and as 'heavy' when armed with guns between 37mm and 45mm. (*Bob Fleming*)

On display at the Central Armed Forces Museum, Moscow is a former Red Army BA-6 heavy armoured car armed with a 45mm main gun. Not seen is the front-hull-mounted 7.62mm machine gun. The vehicle was 15ft (4.57m) long and 6ft 9in (2.05m) wide with a height of 7ft (2.13m). (*Vladimir Yakubov*)

Maximum armour thickness on the BA-3 was 15mm on its turret front and that on the BA-6 was 10mm on its turret front.

There were other versions of the BA-6 built, including one adapted to ride on rails, designated the BA-6ZhD, and another with a smaller and lighter turret, still armed with a 45mm main gun and a coaxial 7.62mm machine gun. A version of the BA-6M armed with a 12.7mm machine gun in place of the 45mm main gun was referred to as the BA-9, of which only several were built due to issues with production of its machine gun. A further modernized version of the BA-6M would result in the BA-10 that featured a maximum armour thickness of 15mm on the front of its redesigned turret. As with the other light and heavy armoured cars, there was a version built to ride on rails known as the BA-10ZhD. Following the BA-10 would be the heavy BA-11 which weighed 17,923lb (8.13mt) with a gasoline-powered engine, and a diesel-powered version known as the BA-11D.

The only armoured car built for the Red Army following the German invasion in 1941 was the BA-64 series. The most numerous model built was designated the BA-64B light armoured car. It had a small open-topped turret mounting a 7.62mm machine gun. A unit of BA-64Bs and their crews is pictured prior to a parade. (*Bob Fleming*)

The Red Army had amassed an inventory of 4,819 armoured cars by the summer of 1941. However, once the German invasion of the Soviet Union took place, their production was halted to concentrate on tank output. Those armoured cars in service, such as the BA-10, would last in service until 1943.

A light armoured car that entered Red Army service during the Second World War was the two-man BA-64, built in small numbers in the latter part of 1942 and into 1943. It was based on the gasoline-powered chassis of the GAZ-64 jeep. The vehicle was armed with a 7.62mm machine gun mounted in an open-topped turret. Maximum armour thickness on the front of the vehicle's turret was 15mm.

An improved version of the BA-64 was designated the BA-64B and entered production in 1943. The 5,952-lb (2.7mt) vehicle featured an open-topped turret with a 7.62mm machine gun. It is estimated that about 11,000 units of the BA-64 series were built from 1941 until 1946. The BA-64 would also see service with the Polish army units serving with the Red Army during the Second World War. Post-war it would be exported to a number of countries friendly to the Soviet Union at different time periods, including China and North Korea.

The Western Allies began supporting the Soviet Union with a wide variety of military equipment beginning in November 1941. Among the items supplied were many tanks and other types of armoured fighting vehicles. Although the countries that comprised the Western Allies found the Communist ideology as distasteful as the Nazis' National Socialism, they embraced the old proverb that 'the enemy of my enemy is my friend'. By supplying the Red Army with as much military equipment as could be spared, the Western Allies knew they would help keep the Soviet Union in the fight and would, in turn, tie down the bulk of the German military ground forces till the end of the war in Europe.

It would be America's factories that supplied the bulk of the tanks and other armoured fighting vehicles that went to the Red Army during the Second World War. Under a programme referred to as 'Lend-Lease', a cross-section of American-designed and built tanks would be shipped overseas in varying numbers through German submarine-infested waters to Russian seaports in the early war period.

Under Lend-Lease, the Red Army would receive 1,336 units of the American-designed and built light tank M3. It was armed with a 37mm main gun and up to five 7.62mm machine guns, albeit firing different types of ammunition to that of

Captured by the United States army from the North Korean army during the Korean War is this BA-64B light armoured car that now resides in the Military Museum of Southern New England. The vehicle formerly belonged to the United States Army Ordnance Museum collection. (*Lorén Hannah*)

Pictured is a knocked-out Komsomolyets Artillery Transporter. Featuring an armoured cab armed with a 7.62mm machine gun, it was intended to tow a 45mm anti-tank and carry its six-man crew who had no armoured protection. A total of 4,401 units of the vehicle were built between 1937 and 1941 in two slightly different versions. (*Bob Fleming*)

their Soviet counterparts. Also sent were 340 units of the slightly-improved light tank M3A1. Both vehicles weighed about 24,000lb (11mt), were powered by gasoline engines and manned by a crew of four. Maximum armour thickness on the front of the turrets of the light tanks M3 and M3A1 was 50mm.

Among the American-designed and built medium tanks that entered into Red Army service were 1,386 units of the diesel-engine-powered M3. The vehicle had a crew of either six or seven men and weighed 61,500lb (28mt). It was armed with a hull-mounted 75mm gun and a turret-mounted 37mm gun plus three 7.62mm machine guns. Maximum armour thickness on the vehicle's front turret was 50mm.

In addition, under Lend-Lease the Red Army took into service 1,990 units of the diesel-engine-powered medium tank M4A2. The 70,200-lb (32mt) vehicle had a crew of five men and was armed with a 75mm main gun and three machine guns; a single 12.7mm and two 7.62mm. Maximum armour thickness on the front of the M4A2 turret was 88mm. Red Army tankers nicknamed the M4 series

The most numerous light tank received by the Red Army under Lend-Lease from the United States was the M3 seen here at Aberdeen Proving Ground, Maryland. The vehicle was powered by an air-cooled radial engine that gave it a maximum road speed of 36 mph. (*Patton Museum*)

tanks they received as *Emcha*, which was a Russian shortening of M4.

The Red Army also received 2,073 units of the improved up-gunned second-generation medium tank M4A2, designated M4A2(76)W. The suffix 'W' represented a main gun storage arrangement that incorporated water to quench propellant fires. The 73,400-lb (33mt) M4A2(76)W had a crew of five men and was armed with a 76mm main gun and three machine guns; as before, a single 12.7mm and two 7.62mm. Maximum armour thickness on the vehicle was 88mm on the turret front.

Fifty-two units of the diesel-engine-powered 3-inch Gun Motor Carriage M10 were also taken into service. This 65,200-lb (30mt) vehicle had a crew of five men. Armament consisted of a 3-inch main gun and a single 12.7mm machine gun. Maximum armour thickness on the vehicle's turret front was 56mm.

In parallel with the various tanks supplied to the Red Army under the Lend-Lease Act there was a wide range of wheeled and half-track armoured vehicles

Another American light tank taken into service by the Red Army during the Second World War was the M3A1. It was an improved version of the M3 light tank, having a gyrostabilizer to allow firing while on the move. The key identifying feature between the two vehicles was the lack of the vehicle commander's cupola on the M3A1. (*Michael Green*)

shipped to the Soviet Union. These would include 3,310 units of the gasoline-engine-powered scout car M3A1. This vehicle weighed 12,400lb (5.6mt) and had a crew of six to eight men. Standard United States army armament consisted of a 12.7mm and a 7.62mm machine gun. Maximum armour protection on the M3A1 was 13mm.

The Red Army would also receive 1,158 American-designed and built open-topped armoured half-tracks. These gasoline-engine-powered vehicles would include 342 units of the half-track car M2 and 603 units of the half-track car M9A1. These open-topped vehicles weighed up to 21,200lb (9.6mt) and had a maximum armour of 16mm on their front hull and a crew of ten men in United States army service, with an armament of a single 12.7mm (.50 calibre) machine gun and up to two 7.62mm (.30 calibre) machine guns.

Also shipped to the Red Army were two examples of the half-track personnel carrier M3 and 401 units of the half-track M5. These vehicles had a twelve-man crew in United States army service and weighed up to 21,500lb (9.7mt). Maximum armour thickness on the M3/M3A1 and the M5 version front hulls was 16mm. Typically, the various versions of these half-track personnel carriers were armed with a single 7.62mm (.30 calibre) or a single 12.7mm (.50 calibre) machine gun. The half-track personnel carriers supplied to the Red Army were typically employed as command vehicles in armoured units.

There was also a half-track-based tank destroyer provided to the Red Army, the Gun Motor Carriage T48. It was based on the chassis of the half-track personnel carrier M3 and armed with a British-designed, American-built 57mm gun. It was mounted in the rear of a modified M3 half-track on a conical structure, designated the 57mm gun mount T5.

Under Lend-Lease the Red Army received a large number of M3 medium tanks from the United States. The vehicle was powered by an air-cooled radial engine that gave it a maximum road speed of 21 mph (33.8 kph). The M3 was 20ft 1in (6.12m) long and 8ft 11in (2.71m) wide with a height of 10ft 3in (3.12m). (*Patton Museum*)

The Red Army was never thrilled with the American-supplied M3 medium tank. They did not like its awkward arrangement of weaponry and its height. It was normally relegated to the infantry support role by the Red Army. Pictured is a United States army M3 taking part in a training exercise. (*Patton Museum*)

Of the 962 T-48s built by the Diamond T Motor Car Company between December 1942 and May 1943, only thirty went to the British army, with 650 going to the Red Army. Of the remaining vehicles, most were eventually converted to the half-track personnel M3A1 configuration for use by the United States army. In Red Army service the T48 was referred to as the SU-57 and would remain in service through to the conclusion of the war in Europe.

The Anti-aircraft Artillery Board of the United States army had a vehicle developed based upon the chassis of the half-track personnel carrier M3. It was armed with a 37mm automatic cannon and two 12.7mm (.50 calibre) air-cooled machine guns. It was referred to as the Multiple Gun Motor Carriage M15A1 and had an open-topped armoured shield around the front and sides of the weapons to protect the gun crew. Some 100 units of the M15A1 were supplied to the Red Army under Lend-Lease.

Another anti-aircraft vehicle known as the Half-Track Multiple Gun Motor Carriage M17 was also supplied to the Red Army under Lend-Lease. It was armed with a power-operated turret designated the M33 that mounted four 12.7mm (.50 calibre) air-cooled machine guns in the open-topped rear hull of the vehicle. Rather than being mounted on the chassis of the half-track personnel

The Red Army was a little more pleased with the two different versions of the diesel-powered M4A2 medium tank it received from the American government under Lend-Lease. Pictured is an early production first-generation unit of the M4A2 armed with a 75mm main gun. (*Patton Museum*)

carrier M3 as was the M15A1, it was mounted on the chassis of the half-track personnel carrier M5 built by the International Harvester Company for foreign aid use only. The entire production run of 1,000 units of the M17 was shipped to the Soviet Union.

The British government also decided early on that it was in their best interests to keep the Red Army in action and supplied it with 3,782 units (of various versions) of the Infantry Tank Mark III, officially nicknamed the 'Valentine'. Armed with either a 40mm or 57mm main gun and a single 7.92mm machine gun, the vehicle weighed approximately 36,000lb (16mt). The tank started off with a crew of three that was pushed up to four men in later production versions. While the initial version of the Valentine had a gasoline-powered engine, subsequent models supplied to the Red Army all had diesel engines. Maximum armour protection on the Valentine series turret front was 65mm.

In addition to the Valentine series, the Red Army received 1,084 units of the Infantry Tank Mark II, officially nicknamed the 'Matilda II'. The four-man vehicle was armed with a 40mm main gun and either one or two 7.92mm machine guns. Weighing in at about 60,000lb (27mt), the tank was powered by a diesel engine and had a maximum armour thickness of 78mm on its turret front.

Another infantry support tank that the British government would supply to the Red Army was officially nicknamed the 'Churchill'. Models provided were the Mark III and Mark IV, both armed with a 57mm main gun. Both gasoline-engine-powered versions were also fitted with two 7.92mm machine guns. The Mark III version of the five-man Churchill tank weighed approximately 87,000lb (39.5mt). Maximum armour thickness on the Churchill Mark III and IV was 102mm on their turret front.

There was also a small shipment of twenty British light tanks designated the

In the foreground of the picture is a first-generation Red Army M4A2 medium tank armed with a 75mm main gun. It is from a later production batch, as it has a glacis sloped at 47 degrees instead of the 57-degree sloped glacis seen on earlier production units of the vehicle. (*Charles Kliment*)

Mark VII sent to the Red Army. In British army service the vehicle was officially nicknamed the 'Tetrarch'. The three-man vehicle was armed with a 40mm main gun and a single 7.92mm machine gun. Weighing in at 16,800lb (7.6mt), the maximum armour thickness on the vehicle's front turret was 16mm.

Besides tanks, the British government sent to the Red Army 2,500 units of the Universal Carrier in whose service they often saw use as a reconnaissance vehicle. The 8,848-lb (4mt) vehicle had crew of four to five men and in British army service was armed with either a 7.7mm light machine gun or a 14.3mm Boys anti-tank rifle. Armour protection on the open-topped Universal Carrier was no more than 10mm.

The most numerous version of the M4A2 medium tank to enter Red Army service was the second-generation model seen here designated the M4A2(76)W. The major external identifying features of this tank were a new, larger turret and a longer-barrelled 76.2mm main gun. (*Charles Kliment*)

During a pause in the fighting, civilians warily look at a second-generation Red Army M4A2(76)W medium tank. The vehicle was 24ft 10in (7.56m) long and 8ft 9in (2.66m) wide with a height of 9ft 9in (2.97m). It had storage space for seventy-one main gun rounds. (*Charles Kliment*)

Among the many armoured fighting vehicles provided to the Red Army by the American government were a small number of open-topped M10 tank destroyers armed with a 3-inch main gun. The vehicle was based on the chassis of the M4A2 medium tank. (*Michael Green*)

Pictured during a training exercise is a United States army M3A1 Scout Car. The Red Army would receive thousands of them under Lend-Lease from the American government. Open-topped and with very thin armour, the vehicle was 18ft 5in (5.61m) long and 6ft 8in (2.03m) wide. (*Patton Museum*)

Some of the crewmen of a Red Army M3A1 Scout Car are shown jumping from their vehicle. This particular vehicle is towing a 76.2mm field gun. It retains the American-supplied 12.7mm (.50 calibre) machine gun nicknamed the 'fifty-cal' or 'Ma Deuce'. (*Bob Fleming*)

The Red Army was supplied via Lend-Lease from the United States a number of armoured half-track models. These included the half-track car M2 seen here with a canvas cover over its open-topped hull. (*Patton Museum*)

The Red Army also took into service the half-track car M9A1 and the half-track personnel carrier M5. Both vehicles were built by the American firm of International Harvester strictly for Lend-Lease customers. An identifying feature of these vehicles is the rounded rear hull corners as seen on the M5 pictured here. (*Patton Museum*)

Another Lend-Lease armoured half-track acquired by the Red Army was designated the 57mm gun motor carriage T48 and is seen here. It consisted of a modified half-track personnel M3 mounting a 57mm anti-tank gun in a fixed forward-firing position with limited traverse. (*Charles Kliment*)

The United States government provided the Red Army with two different types of anti-aircraft armoured half-tracks. The Half-Track Combination Gun Motor Carriage M15A1 pictured here was armed with a single 37mm automatic cannon and two 12.7mm (.50 calibre) machine guns and the Half-Track Multiple Gun Motor Carriage M17 was armed with four 12.7mm (.50 calibre) machine guns. (*Patton Museum*)

On display at Kubinka is a British-designed Valentine Infantry Tank Mark III. It is armed with a 57mm main gun. The Red Army would be supplied with both British- and Canadian-built units of the vehicle that came in various versions and had different main guns fitted. (*Vladimir Yakubov*)

Also provided by the British government to the Red Army was the Matilda II Infantry Tank armed with a 40mm main gun. Powered by two diesel engines, it had a top speed on level roads of 15 mph (24 kph). This particular vehicle is on display at the military museum located at the Canadian Forces Base, Borden, Canada. (*Paul Hannah*)

A well-armoured but poorly-armed tank supplied to the Red Army was the British-designed and built Churchill Infantry Tank. Pictured is a Mark III version armed with a 57mm main gun in a welded turret, which belongs to the United States Army Ordnance Museum collection. (*Michael Green*)

Shipped to the Soviet Union in very small numbers for use by the Red Army was the Light Tank Mark VII seen here. It was officially nicknamed the 'Tetrarch' and was intended as a reconnaissance vehicle. It could reach a maximum road speed of 40 mph (64 kph). (*Bob Fleming*)

A Red Army Universal Carrier is armed with a Russian anti-tank rifle and a British-built and supplied .303 Bren light machine gun. The vehicle had a length of 12ft 4in (3.75m) and a width of 6ft 11in (2.10m), but a height of only 5ft 3in (1.60m). (*Patton Museum*)

A column of whitewashed Red Army Universal Carriers is pictured carrying a unit of infantry wearing snow suits into battle. The gasoline engine in the vehicle could propel it up to a maximum road speed of 32 mph (51 kph) and gave it an operational range of about 160 miles (257km). (*Bob Fleming*)

As with the German army, the Red Army was not averse to using their opponent's tanks and armoured fighting vehicles if the opportunity presented itself. Pictured is a captured German StuG III assault gun that has been whitewashed and given a Red Star and also covered with some patriotic slogans for good measure. (*Bob Fleming*)